THE VENETIAN

Borgo Press Books by ALEXANDRE DUMAS

Anthony
The Barricade at Clichy
Bathilda
Caligula
The Corsican Brothers
The Count of Monte Cristo, Part One: The Betrayal of Edmond Dantès
The Count of Monte Cristo, Part Two: The Resurrection of Edmond Dantès
The Count of Monte Cristo, Part Three: The Rise of Monte Cristo
The Count of Monte Cristo, Part Four: The Revenge of Monte Cristo
A Fairy Tale (with Adolphe de Leuven and Léon Lhérie)
The Gold Thieves
The Last of the Three Musketeers; or, The Prisoner of the Bastille (Musketeers #3)
Lorenzino
The Mohican's War
Napoléon Bonaparte
Queen Margot
Richard Darlington (with Prosper Dinaux)
Sylvandire
The Three Musketeers (Musketeers #1)
The Three Musketeers—Twenty Years Later (Musketeers #2)
The Tower of Nesle (with Frédéric Gaillardet)
The Two Dianas (with Paul Meurice)
Urbain Grandier and the Devils of Loudon
The Venetian (with Auguste Anicet-Bourgeois)
The Whites and the Blues
The Widow's Husband; and, Porthos in Search of an Outfit
Young Louix XIV

RELATED DRAMAS:

The Queen's Necklace, by Pierre Decourcelle
The Seed of the Musketeers, by Paul de Kock & Guénée (Musketeers #5)
The San Felice, by Maurice Drack
The Son of Porthos the Musketeer, by Émile Blavet (Musketeers #4)
A Summer Night's Dream, by Adolphe de Leuven and Joseph-Bernard Rosier
The Widow's Husband; and, Porthos in Search of an Outfit: Two Dumasian Comedies, edited by Frank J. Morlock

THE VENETIAN

A PLAY IN FIVE ACTS

ALEXANDRE DUMAS & AUGUSTE ANICET-BOURGEOIS

Adapted from the Novel, *The Bravo*, by James Fenimore Cooper; Translated by Frank J. Morlock

THE BORGO PRESS
MMXII

THE VENETIAN

Copyright © 2004, 2012 by Robert Reginald

FIRST BORGO PRESS EDITION

Published by Wildside Press LLC

www.wildsidebooks.com

DEDICATION

*To Sami Caldwell,
my good friend in San Miguel*

CONTENTS

CAST OF CHARACTERS	9
ACT I, Scene 1	11
ACT I, Scene 2	31
ACT II, Scene 3	47
ACT II, Scene 4	73
ACT III, Scene 5	87
ACT IV, Scene 6	113
ACT IV, Scene 7	133
ACT V, Scene 8	153
ABOUT THE AUTHOR	183

CAST OF CHARACTERS

The Bravo

Salfieri

Count de Bellamonte

Luigi

Maffeo

Marquis de Ruffo

A Senator

A Bailiff

A Gondolier

Theodora

Violetta

Michelemma

Two Masked Ladies

ACT I
SCENE 1

The Proscribed.

The interior of the Bravo's house, in a secluded section of Venice. Open window giving on the gulf lit by the moon.

BRAVO

So, Milord, the visit you are paying me this evening is to speak to me of the affairs of Your Excellency and not those of the Republic.

COUNT

It's a service that I have to ask of you, and I don't doubt for a moment that—

BRAVO

I will be at your orders, right? As I am those of the Council of Ten.

COUNT

Of which I am one—don't forget.

BRAVO

What can I do for Your Excellency?

COUNT

A lot.

BRAVO

I am listening.

COUNT

I'm in love.

BRAVO

With the Courtesan, Theodora, I know.

COUNT

And how's that?

BRAVO

A week ago, at the foot of the Lion column, where I habitually hang out, I saw you pass by, as a member of a cortege which ordinarily accompanies the Venetian to church.

COUNT

Yes, it's true. I had, like all there is noble and elegant in Venice, placed myself at the feet of this woman as strange as she is beautiful, a modern Aspasia, who intends to see at her knees all the celebrities of her century, to adorn herself with lovers as other women adorn themselves with jewels. Theodora overwhelmed me with her good graces—but this easy happiness tired me, and I've discovered behind the Bridge of La Paglia, facing the house of the Gondolier Luigi, a diamond.

BRAVO

There are few diamonds in Venice which are not for sale, Your Excellency, is rich and can buy the one he desires.

COUNT

She's refused all my offers.

BRAVO

Double them.

COUNT

No use—I have to deal with an old geezer who is guarding her—who is her father or something like that—He's made of honor, delicacy, rigid virtue.

BRAVO

(with irony)

The wretch!

COUNT

And he's gone so far as to tell me that if I reappear in the street, although he's old and a plebeian, and I am young and of the nobility—he will find a way to get rid of me.

BRAVO

(with irony)

The insolent.

COUNT

I cannot involve myself with this man, you understand?

BRAVO

Surely—these sorts of folks ought to be very happy when a lord of race and birth, like you, deigns to covet his wife or his daughter; that dishonors them but that ennobles them.

COUNT

Well! Now that's what he fails to understand.

BRAVO

The beast.

COUNT

Then I thought of you to rid me of this man: arrived only a few days ago in Venice, he doesn't know anyone and public rumor announces that he raised this delicious creature from charity, and she has, outside this old geezer, neither friends nor relatives under heaven.

Now the young girl is orphaned; the Republic, which is a good mother, adopts the abandoned child. A powerful man, a member of the Council of Ten, I, for example, I take responsibility, for the love of Humanity of placing her in a convent—I'll pay her dowry—I'll make a gift of a Raphael or a Titian to the Chapel of the monastery and the young girl is mine.

BRAVO

It's a marvelous scheme, Milord, and I don't see anything which is preventing this plan from succeeding for you have without doubt for me an order from the Council.

COUNT

What do you mean?

BRAVO

Which enjoins me to rid Venice of an old geezer suspected of virtue, forearmed with delicacy and very religiously determined to guard the honor of a young girl!

COUNT

Why haven't you understood me?

BRAVO

On the contrary, Milord, I have understood you and perfectly. Why you told me the first, what you wanted and it's my turn now to tell you what I want, an order from the Council.

COUNT

(pulling out a purse full of money)

Wait, here it is.

BRAVO

(pushing it away)

The Republic is magnificent, Milord; it rewards richly those who serve it, it covers with gold the weapon each time it spills blood—it's a jealous mistress to whom I do not wish to be unfaithful—I want an official order—

COUNT

Why such a scruple on your part astonishes me, confounds me.

BRAVO

I have a bargain in blood with the Republic—it's true Count Bellamonte—your father was a member of the Council when this bargain was imposed on me—as for him, he knew what motive had make me put this dagger in hand and this mask on my face; your father would not have come to me making the demand you are—I want an order.

COUNT

But if I obtain that order you won't have committed one less murder.

BRAVO

For which I will answer to men—but which the Council of Ten will join me in answering before God.

COUNT

Well; since you absolutely must have an order you will get it. The old man is coming from Genoa, Genoa is at war with the

Republic, and that man that no one knows here is without any doubt a spy of the Doria. I shall have the order and I will have it nailed to your door as is the custom of this tribunal.

Think now, that it will be no longer be to me, but to the Council, that you will render an account of your obedience.

BRAVO

That's fine.

COUNT

Goodbye—don't forget—behind the bridge of Paglia, facing the house of the gondolier Luigi.

BRAVO

Goodbye, Count.

(The Count leaves.)

BRAVO

(alone)

The day is not yet over it seems. The Republic is very hard to serve. No matter, let's profit by the hour that is left to me.

(removing his mask which he hangs on a hook)

Infernal mask!

(removing his dagger which he places on a table)

Cursed dagger!

Which makes itself a part of me—as if the hand of God had imprinted the mask on my face and the other nailed to my belt.

Oh! Let my mouth breathe—now I am a man like all other men—ah!

(he stretches out, overcome, on the bed)

(Salfieri appears outside and jumps with agility into the room.)

BRAVO

Who goes there?

SALFIERI

Greetings to your Lordship.

BRAVO

(rushing to his dagger)

Who are you?

SALFIERI

A man against whom you have no need to draw this dagger—for you can kill me with a word—I'm proscribed.

BRAVO

And why come in like this, thorough the window?

SALFIERI

Because you probably would not have opened the door to me.

BRAVO

What do you want?

SALFIERI

An asylum for the night.

BRAVO

And if I refuse, what will happen?

SALFIERI

Only something very simple, six years ago, I left Venice under weight of a death warrant—a motive more powerful than my life has brought me back.

A ship let me off on the beach—and if I get back to it in an hour, it is my vessel. I no longer know a single friend in Venice.

Your protection is my life—your refusal is my death. If you refuse me, we are both young—you have a dagger—I have one. The chances are equal—if you kill me, I have no need of asylum tonight; if I kill you, my refuge is found. I no more fear sleeping near a dead enemy than beside a living friend.

BRAVO

And if, on the contrary, I protect you?

SALFIERI

You will have done an immense service to a man who will remember it eternally.

BRAVO

(extending his hand)

Put it there.

SALFIERI

Thanks.

BRAVO

Now, I am going to close this window for I am no longer alone.

(coming back)

Well?

SALFIERI

Well, my host—I am at your orders. Do you want to stay up, I'll stay up. Do you want to sleep—toss yourself on this bed and I will toss myself on this cloak—are you disposed to do for me more than you have done so far? I will tell you what brings me to Venice—for what purpose I have come—what woman I am pursuing—what man I am seeking—then, if you cause me to speak to his man, or to meet this woman, you will be more to me than a protector, than a friend, you will be a god.

BRAVO

Speak and what I can do I will do.

SALFIERI

I'm exiled over a political affair, there's only one thing that can make an exile forget his country—it's love. Proscribed by the Republic of Venice, I found exile in the Republic of Genoa—by chance, I met a young girl, I loved her, she loved me, I forgot everything.

BRAVO

That's really a youthful head and a youthful heart—that's really love.

SALFIERI

Yes, yes—for six months I had only one thought—her—all my days were spent waiting for night, because, guarded as she was, only at night could I see her. Then I crossed over the garden wall. Confident and pure as a Madonna, she came to open up for me—and I, timid and childishly amorous, I lay at her feet seeking my life in her eyes—forgetting the past which was slipping away without her, happy in the present I felt was mine—confident in a future I believed was ours—

BRAVO

That's really the way the mad hours of youth are spent, I remember myself—

SALFIERI

One night I came as usual—I found open the door that Violetta ordinarily opened to me—

BRAVO

(shivering)

Violetta.

SALFIERI

That was her name—it brings back some memory—?

BRAVO

I, too, I loved a woman named Violetta—

SALFIERI

You—!

BRAVO

For her I left Venice. Venice that I never expected to see again and that to my misfortune I have seen—Oh! But that was sixteen years ago—and that woman is dead—it's the first time in sixteen years I've heard that name mentioned—and it seized my heart—continue—

SALFIERI

I went up the stairs—I entered her room. I called excitedly. I ran to the room of the old man at risk of meeting him—it was deserted like that of Violetta—fragments of torn letters half burned were on the ground—I put them together. I found an order—given by, I don't know whom—to this man—to immediately escort the young girl who was confided to him—where? The name of the city wasn't there—she was gone. The old man had taken her away. I came back to Violetta's room—furious, desperate—asking loudly for indications, a trace—suddenly my eyes were fixed on a mirror—and Violetta's hand had written with a diamond the sole word, "Venice"—then I forgot everything: proscriptions, arrest, death—the scaffold—I left and here I am.

BRAVO

And now what you are counting on doing with the weak information that you possess—in an immense city where you cannot show your face—in the midst of an incessantly active police—with all their eyes opened—some agent of whom perhaps already knows of your arrival—?

SALFIERI

Yes, yes, I know all that—thus my plan resembles my position—desperate—Listen, I have only told you I was coming to Venice to pursue a woman and to seek a man—the woman that I am pursing is—Violetta.

BRAVO

And the man you are seeking?

SALFIERI

It's the Bravo.

BRAVO

Huh!

SALFIERI

Do you know him?

BRAVO

And who in Venice does not know this man? Only the Council of Ten can reply to that question.

SALFIERI

Where can one meet him?

BRAVO

On the Piazetta—everyday—at the foot of the Lion column—sad, black and motionless, a type of living scaffold—eternally executed on the public square of Venice.

SALFIERI

And what do they say about this man?

BRAVO

A thousand different things.

SALFIERI

But what is the truth on his account?

BRAVO

God alone and he could tell it—all others are mistaken.

SALFIERI

But in your opinion?

BRAVO

I don't have one about him.

SALFIERI

That's well enough. I will find him. I always have three ways of making a man do what I wish.

BRAVO

Which are?

SALFIERI

Prayer: an appeal to his humanity; money: an appeal to his avarice; threat: an appeal to his weakness.

BRAVO

Prayer—the Bravo has heard more prayers than Saint Ambrose who is the patron of the city—and I don't know of a single one that has softened him—money—the Bravo has received enough from the Republic to purchase a palace if he was ambitious to sleep in a marble chamber—threats—the Bravo—by force of making them has lost the habit of hearing them—

SALFIERI

But does nothing human remain in the heart of that man?

BRAVO

Nothing.

SALFIERI

Doesn't he even have a mother?

BRAVO

He had one, and God took her from him in an hour of wrath.

SALFIERI

No mistress?

BRAVO

He had one, and he killed her in a moment of jealousy.

SALFIERI

No father?

(Bravo lowers his head on his breast and his face takes on an expression of sorrow and somber reverie.)

SALFIERI

(continuing)

Well! I will adjure him in the name of his father—yes, tonight—this very night, I must see him.

BRAVO

And what will you ask on seeing him?

SALFIERI

That, my host—that's my secret.

BRAVO

Nothing can dissuade you from searching for this man?

SALFIERI

Nothing—for I have no hope except in him.

BRAVO

You will see him then.

SALFIERI

Who will make me see him?

BRAVO

I will.

SALFIERI

And when will that be?

(Three raps on the door.)

BRAVO

Wait, I am going to tell you.

(He goes to the door and finds the order of the Council that's just been nailed there. He comes forward holding it in his hand, examines it, then takes his cloak and hides his mask and dagger under it.)

BRAVO

(aside)

They signed it.

SALFIERI

Well—

BRAVO

In an hour—

SALFIERI

And where will I find him?

BRAVO

Behind the bridge of La Paglia—facing the house of the Gondolier Luigi.

SALFIERI

In an hour—?

BRAVO

In an hour.

SALFIERI

That's fine—I will be there.

(The Bravo leaves and Salfieri follows him with his eyes.)

CURTAIN

ACT I
SCENE 2

Near the audience on each side, two gothic doors, vaulted and projecting into the street. Farther back two alleyways facing one another. Farther back the bridge of La Paglia. In the distance the Grand Canal.

Night.

The Bravo is leaning against the door of Luigi; he is coming from the rear with his gondola.

LUIGI

(singing)

Here's the mad breeze
Which has kept whispering to me
Michelemma (repeat)

This name sails in the air
And keeps pursing me—
Michelemma (repeat)

For my gondola—days—
To my bedstead at night.

(He docks, attaches his gondola to the ring and continues to sing.)

LUIGI

Leave your halo
In paradise, my angel
Michelemma (repeat)
Descend, my idol,
To the parts where I am.
Michelemma

For my gondola—days
To my bedside at night.

(The Bravo emerges as Luigi approaches his door.)

BRAVO

Silence! Luigi!

LUIGI

The Bravo! Lord! Lord! I haven't done anything to the Republic.

BRAVO

Listen to me.

LUIGI

I'm listening.

BRAVO

You are going to go into your home.

LUIGI

I'm going to go in.

BRAVO

If someone knocks, you won't open.

LUIGI

No.

BRAVO

If you hear some screams—you won't come out—

LUIGI

No—

BRAVO

And if by chance, in your home, some light is burning that shines on the street, you are going to extinguish it—

LUIGI

Immediately.

BRAVO

They're opening that door, that's fine. Go inside.

(Luigi goes inside; one hears a locking of a door within. The Bravo moves away by one of the alleys—the door facing that of Luigi opens. Maffeo emerges first followed by Theodora and

Violetta.)

MAFFEO

Pardon, Madame, I thought I heard talking.

THEODORA

See—

MAFFEO

I am mistaken—there is no one.

VIOLETTA

And when will I see you again, Madame—?

THEODORA

My visits give you pleasure, my child?

VIOLETTA

Yes, I am happy when you come, you seem to love me so much, Madame, me, a poor, abandoned orphan. Pardon, Maffeo, I am speaking of my mother and not of you.

THEODORA

Your mother! My child don't ever accuse her without knowing what motives separated you from her—perhaps, she suffers more than you from your absence—and think that, near God, it's a terrible accusation that a daughter is making against her mother.

VIOLETTA

Oh! I am not accusing her of andonment, Madame! I am weeping over her absence.

THEODORA

(taking her in her arms with distraction)

Kiss me!

MAFFEO

(low)

You are forgetting, Madame, that it is dangerous for Signora Violetta.

THEODORA

Yes, yes, you are right. Go back inside, my child—the night air of Venice is fatal to youthful and fresh faces like yours—go back inside.

VIOLETTA

And when will I see you again, Madame?

THEODORA

Tomorrow I cannot come; the day after—

VIOLETTA (kissing her hand)

How good you are to love me—!

(She goes in and shuts the door.)

THEODORA

Oh! Maffeo! What a sweet and ravishing creature! And how I reproach myself now for having kept her separated from me for so long.

MAFFEO

I told you in my letters, Madame, that you were depriving yourself of a great happiness.

THEODORA

Yes, but I was trembling that my funeral celebrity, of which I was so proud before having seen my daughter, would reach her! A pure daughter is a terrible judge for a mother like me! Call Luigi, Maffeo.

MAFFEO

(going to rap on Luigi's door)

But this secret—you will reveal it to her one day?

THEODORA

Yes, yes—in six months, in a year—I will take her to Naples, to Rome, to France, perhaps, no matter where, so long as it is far enough from Venice for the name of Theodora not to be widely known. I will confess everything to her there—and if you are still with us, Maffeo, you will join with me, you will tell her I was as pure as she—that you knew me, loved and worthy of being loved, you will tell her that the one I was going to marry in a moment of jealousy—oh! Very unjust jealousy!

Oh—without this child that I carried in my breast, without this child who today makes all my hope of the future, how much I would have regretted that Giovanni's dagger had not penetrated deeper.

MAFFEO

Yes, you say that here, Madame, in a secluded and somber street of Venice, alone with me, all distraught again with the embarrassments of your daughter, but in your palace on the Piazetta, in the midst of flaming torches, resplendant diamonds, intoxicating praise, with all this youth hanging at your feet like those of a queen—and who tell you day and night with a thousand voices—Theodora! Theodora you are beautiful.

Oh! Wow! Don't you applaud that Giovanna had a hand so unsure—and that wound that he thought mortal was so quickly healed and left such a slight scar—

THEODORA

Yes, yes, I confess it—this life has its delights, its pleasures, but it's not happiness—well—your Luigi is not coming.

(Maffeo raps again)

Do you know, Maffeo, in order that such things will not happen, I will take this man into my service; I am too well known in Venice for this gondolier who dwells opposite your house, not to suspect who this disguised woman is—better to pay for his silence, I think, than to fear his indiscretion. But what to do if he doesn't come.

MAFFEO

I am going to row you myself, Madame, Luigi's gondola is

moored in a secret place that I know, and if you want to accept me for your conductor—

THEODORA

Very well—Only you ought to have found this expedient right away—the air coming from the gulf is frigid and dangerous tonight—tomorrow I will be pale.

MAFFEO

(moving away)

Ah! That beauty which you take so much care of is fatal to you, Madame!

THEODORA

Indeed, I care for it, Maffeo, and as jealous as I am of it, it will go one day—and then it will be time to—

MAFFEO

To think of God—right? But won't it be too late for God to think of you?

(he gets into the gondola, Theodora follows him)

BRAVO

(entering by the street on the right)

That's him! There's the old geezer who is giving himself up—what I always notice in the admirable order of Providence, is that everything conspires to facilitate an evil deed and to prevent a good one.

Is there then a God for Murder?

SALFIERI

(entering by the right who heard the last words)

Yes—men call him Satan.

BRAVO

No doubt you are one of his apostles you who know his name as well?

SALFIERI

Not yet. But I am coming to Venice to enlist in his ranks.

BRAVO

What master have you chosen?

SALFIERI

You.

BRAVO

You know who I am?

SALFIERI

You are the Bravo—

BRAVO

And you are coming this way to me, at night, without fear.

SALFIERI

I had one: That of not meeting you—

BRAVO

Well—here I am.

SALFIERI

(aside)

That voice.

(aloud)

Let me look at you first.

BRAVO

Look—

SALFIERI

Yes—there indeed is the man with the black mask; this strange spectacle finally that was depicted to me, so you are the magical man—before whom all doors open, in whose presence all laughter ceases, in whose presence all veils fall; you can take by the arm whoever you wish, lead him where you please, enter and leave Venice freely at any hour of the night, you can do this—

BRAVO

I can do it.

SALFIERI

And you owe this privilege?

VIOLETTA

To my mask and my dagger.

SALFIERI

And the one who wears them will have the same power?

BRAVO

Yes, if he has the same courage.

SALFIERI

Will you loan them to me?

BRAVO

What are you saying?

SALFIERI

I am saying to you that I must have it at all costs for two days, your mask and your dagger—for it's necessary that all gates open to me too, all the bailiffs move aside, all veils fall—it's necessary that I can take whoever I wish by the arm—lead him where it pleases me, enter and leave Venice freely at any hour of the night or day—and for that indeed you see your mask and dagger are necessary to me.

BRAVO

But for those two days, you will be what I have been for so long—the terror and anathema of Venice!

SALFIERI

That's all right.

BRAVO

During those two days you will do what I do?

SALFIERI

I will do it.

BRAVO

If I get an order from the Council of Ten?

SALFIERI

I will execute it.

BRAVO

And if this order directs a murder?

SALFIERI

Enough! Only your mask can hide in Venice the face of a proscribed! Only your dagger can defend him or avenge him—at all cost, I want them.

BRAVO

But do you know what it's like to look at creation through this mask? Do you know that it darkens everything, that no more air can reach your breast, that no ray of sunlight can warm your face? Do you know that you can only remove it when you are alone, and that each time you take it off, you will find your eyes more hollow and your face more pale—do you know that?

SALFIERI

I know it—

BRAVO

Do you know that on the day of the Last Judgment, even if you wore this mask only for an hour, if it was a bloody hour, the angel of death will come grab you by your face and that you will only look at God sideways.

SALFIERI

(stamping his foot)

But give me this mask and this dagger.

BRAVO

My dagger—you think, possibly that it is a hornet which strikes bravely by day? No, no—it's a weapon of the night, a weapon of treachery—

SALFIERI

No matter!

BRAVO

No sooner will you have it at your side than you will have to draw it from its scabbard and strike.

(noticing the gondola rowed by Maffeo)

To strike an old man—an old man who's the same age as your father—a voice that resembles that of your father—white hair like that of your father.

(gesture by Salfieri)

You will weaken?

SALFIERI

Ah! Think that at each step I take in this city I can be recognized. Yet, one more time, and for the last time, can you and will you give me what I'm asking for?

BRAVO

Fool!

(after a silence)

Yes, I can do it—if you wish it—for only two men in Venice know the face of the Bravo—two men alone would be able to say, seeing him without his mask, it's him—one of these men is the head of the Council of Ten—and he's away for a week—the other—

(aside)

It's a way to save him, perhaps.

(aloud)

Listen—you are proscribed and if I refuse you—I ruin you—for how long am I making this horrible loan to you?

SALFIERI

For two days—

BRAVO

Then swear to me that within two days you will return to me this mask and this dagger—that in two days you won't tell anyone either who I am or who you are—swear to me—on what you hold most sacred.

SALFIERI

On the wounds of Christ, I swear it to you—

BRAVO

I accept your oath; listen midnight is striking.

SALFIERI

Well! In two days and when midnight strikes—

BRAVO

Not an hour, not a minute—not a second before.

SALFIERI

Not before the last hour has struck as it is striking and may not be extinguished as it is extinguishing.

(The Bravo goes to the back of the stage, descends the steps of the quay, disappearing before the eyes of the spectators, then, an instant later one hears a groan and the noise of a body falling in the water—meanwhile Salfieri remains motionless in front of the stage.)

BRAVO

(returning his naked, embloodied dagger in hand)

You still want them?

(removing his mask)

Here they are.

SALFIERI

(taking his hand)

Thanks, mine host.

BRAVO

(starting to leave, then stopping)

In two days, at midnight.

SALFIERI

In two days at midnight.

CURTAIN

ACT II
SCENE 3

The young girl.

The Piazetta—at the left, near the audience the Portico of Saint Mark—Much further to the rear part of the stairway of Giants can be seen. Almost opposite, the column of the Lion. To the right—the Palace of Theodora. The rear represents a view of the Grand Canal seen from the grand square of Saint Mark.

BRAVO

(alone, richly dressed as a Dalmatian Nobleman)

Yes, I recognize you, fresh breeze of the Apennines, to this orangey savor that you bring us from Florence, and still it was so long ago that I had forgotten it, since my fatal return to Venice. You struck on my mask and on my face. Oh! I recognize you, Venice of my youthful and happy years—here indeed is your Ducal palace, your stairway of giants, your Lion of Saint Mark, the cutting sword, with wings spread—it seems to me I'm an exile who once again places his foot on native soil, a son who returns to the paternal house.

(people began to circulate)

Venice! Oh! I am going to pass through your streets without

leaving a trace of blood. Now I am going to mix in the crowd without being cursed by it. Because if I recognize you, you don't recognize me, Venice! I know all your secrets and you are unaware of mine. Oh! I am going to live for two days the life of happy me. Future! Past—bloody demons who march before and after me—get away! Get away! Let me breathe a little.

Now that this odious mask no longer weighs on my face—I was capable of imploring pity already—I was capable of making gold shine—yes, since yesterday, a hope has come to me—and tomorrow, perhaps this evening, I will learn if God wants to be merciful to me at last. A fool has taken my place—thus as I am used to doing he awaits at the Ducal Palace the Orders of the Council. During these two days they won't have any to give him, I hope—and as for me, during these two days—indifference on my face, laughter on my lip, I can attempt anything—yes, anything to snatch from the palace prison the pledge which answers for the Bravo—

A GONDOLIER

And he was like this on the ground—on the quay.

LUIGI

Oh! My God yes—like a dog—

A MAN

And dead?

LUIGI

Oh! Killed roughly—the blow was given as if for a young man who would have had sixty years to live.

A MAN

Poor old geezer—it's an infamous murder—a murder of a Turk and not of a Christian.

ANOTHER

And you are sure that it was again this cursed Bravo!

LUIGI

Yes, for sure, because if I'd got there a moment sooner, I'd have saved Maffeo.

ALL

Really?

LUIGI

I was the first to get there—and when the Bravo saw me—

A MAN

He took flight?

LUIGI

No, not exactly—no—I ought to say that he even showed a certain courage—but it's all the same, he must really hold a grudge against me.

BRAVO

(laughing)

Not at all, Luigi, you are mistaken.

LUIGI

Huh, Excellency.

BRAVO

I am saying that far from wishing you ill, the Bravo owes you a reward and I don't doubt that he will give it to you at the first opportunity.

LUIGI

Why's that?

BRAVO

All effort deserves a reward and you submitted to his orders blindly.

LUIGI

Me?

BRAVO

Certainly, you went into your house as he told you to go in; you didn't come out because he told you not to leave; and you hastened to blow out the only light from the house shining on the street, so that the night was very dark, and that no indiscreet window looked on the murder—

LUIGI

(recoiling)

If you are not Satan, who are you then?

BRAVO

I am a Dalmatian noble born on the banks of Cattaco whose inhabitants are as everyone knows—gifted with the power of magic.

LUIGI

Holy Mary—protect us.

MICHELEMMA

(entering)

Luigi! Luigi! Good news.

LUIGI

Ah! There you are, little olive. What is making you so happy?

MICHELEMMA

The news I am bringing you. I am coming to tell you that from today you are going to be part of the house of Signora Theodora—in the job of confidential gondolier—

LUIGI

Son of a gun!

MICHELEMMA

Well? Are you happy?

LUIGI

Yes, certainly, for my body which finds a very agreeable position—but I swear to you I am devilishly uneasy about my soul.

MICHELEMMA

Oh! Pooh! My God! There's that Marquis again.

LUIGI

What Marquis?

MICHELEMMA

The Marquis de Ruffo—it's me he's looking for.

LUIGI

What do you mean it's you he's looking for?

MICHELEMMA

Oh, don't worry, jealous one—it's not for me that he's looking.

LUIGI

He did well.

MICHELEMMA

What's that mean?

LUIGI

Because if someone allowed himself to cast his eyes on you—

MICHELEMMA

What then?

LUIGI

He would have an affair with a man who has for a long while sought the opportunity—

MICHELEMMA

Well, my friend, it's presenting itself.

LUIGI

Huh!

MICHELEMMA

And at the same time you will give proof to your new employer a proof of your devotion—for which she will be very grateful.

LUIGI

Explain yourself!

MICHELEMMA

That young lord is pursuing the Signora Theodora at all hours, in all places.

LUIGI

And what's he want from her?

MICHELEMMA

Her love.

LUIGI

Is he rich?

MICHELEMMA

Yes.

LUIGI

Then he will buy it.

MICHELEMMA

Yes, but it's not only that—heavens—here he is!

(The Marquis de Ruffo enters seeming to be looking for someone.)

LUIGI

Ah, I find he's very nice, this young Lord.

MICHELEMMA

What do you mean?

LUIGI

That he seems very noble and that your mistress is very wrong to disdain him.

MICHELEMMA

But that's no concern of ours, from the moment she orders us—for I say "us" now that you are in her service—from the moment she orders us to rid her of an importunate.

LUIGI

Your mistress has no right to prevent a gentleman from as noble a house as that the Marquis de Ruffo comes from—

MICHELEMMA

Do you want me to say something to you, Luigi?

LUIGI

Say something.

MICHELEMMA

And that I speak to you frankly?

LUIGI

Frankly.

MICHELEMMA

You are a poltroon.

LUIGI

Me!

MICHELEMMA

Yes, you—and if someone wants to offer me his arm and rid me of that young man I will give him what I would have given to you.

LUIGI

And what would you have given me?

MICHELEMMA

A kiss—just let someone give me his arm and you will see if I keep my word.

BRAVO

(going to her and offering her his hand)

There's what you are asking for, child.

MICHELEMMA

What, you lordship would consent?

BRAVO

Certainly—

MICHELEMMA

Thanks—

LUIGI

(moving away)

Again this devil of a man!

RUFFO

(moving away)

Ah! I observe her at last.

MICHELEMMA

He's coming to us.

BRAVO

Let's spare him half the road.

MARQUIS

Ah! There are you are at last, my charming—

MICHELEMMA

My God—Sir—will you keep tormenting me forever?

MARQUIS

Forever, until you undertake to deliver this letter to the Signora.

MICHELEMMA

But, sir, I cannot; you know it very well.

MARQUIS

Why?

MICHELEMMA

I already told you that my mistress has forbidden me—

MARQUIS

And why did she forbid you?

MICHELEMMA

Because she doesn't like you.

MARQUIS

And why doesn't she like me?

BRAVO

Because you are a conceited puppy.

MARQUIS

(taking a step back)

Signor.

BRAVO

(advancing a step)

Marquis.

MICHELEMMA

(letting go the Bravo's arm)

Oh! My God!

MARQUIS

(half drawing his sword)

You've said words there that make a sword emerge from it scabbard.

BRAVO

And I'm going to tell you others which will make it hurry back in—Marquis de Ruffo, your uncle, the Senator, who was so rich and of whom you are the sole heir—died very quickly and was buried very promptly.

MARQUIS

What are you saying?

BRAVO

I am saying that if the mortician had looked under his left breast.

MARQUIS

Silence! In the name of heaven.

(he puts back his sword)

BRAVO

I told you so.

MARQUIS

Why who are you then, to know such secrets, my Master?

BRAVO

A rich merchant from the Gulf of Perisque—who came to Venice from Baghdad and Jerusalem; and who during the nights of the journey amused myself by reading in the stars.

(turning)

Michelemma.

MICHELEMMA

My lord—

BRAVO

Don't worry, you have no more to fear from this young man.

MICHELEMMA

Here's my Mistress—excuse me.

BRAVO

Ah! The beautiful Theodora—the Aspasia of our time, who takes the century of Julius II for that of Pericles—Venice for Athens and Bellamonte for Alcibiades.

(Theodora, Bellamonte, and young Lords enter.)

THEODORA

(in a nonchalant, jesting manner)

Why, it's truly a chivalrous love—yours is, Signor Count.

BELLAMONTE

You are laughing, Madame, that's very cruel—to laugh over a passionate love that is driving me mad.

THEODORA

(leaning on his arm)

My dear Count, the case arises, we will beg Ariosto, who is our friend, to make you saddle the hippogriff, and give you a passport for the moon, but I warn you, Count, that I am difficult regarding evidence of madness.

BELLAMONTE

And why's that?

THEODORA

Because I have been spoiled. See this ring—

BELLAMONTE

It's a simple engagement ring.

THEODORA

Yes, but it's the ring of the marriage of the Doge and the Sea. Three years ago, I was on one of the gondolas closest to the Bucentaure, when the Doge threw this ring into the Adriatic. It came to me to say that whoever brought me this ring. I would grant what he asked of me.

At that moment I heard a shout. A young Frenchman whose ship touched mine fell into the sea—twice I saw him reappear and sink, then a third time finally he came to the surface swimming with one hand and with the other displaying to me the ring I wanted.

BELLAMONTE

And this ring?

THEODORA

I kept mine, and I no longer recall what he asked of me when he brought it to me that night. But what he asked, I know that he obtained.

BELLAMONTE

Well! Madame, put my love to some test of the same sort.

THEODORA

(pointing to the Bravo)

There's a Dalmatian nobleman wearing a beautiful Mexican chain around his neck.

BELLAMONTE

(going to the Bravo)

Greetings to Your Excellency.

BRAVO

Greetings.

BELLAMONTE

(touching the chain)

Your Excellency possesses a precious jewel.

BRAVO

Yes, it's a gold chain that I bought in Seville—it came from Christopher Columbus who sold it to his jailor to obtain bread less black and water more pure.

BELLAMONTE

Christopher Columbus doesn't matter much to me—but I need this chain. Can it be paid for with gold or with steel—with the purse or with the sword?

BRAVO

Neither the one nor the other, milord, this chain I'm keeping for the Count de Bellamonte.

BELLAMONTE

You are saying?

BRAVO

That he asked me to give it to a young girl who lives behind the Bridge of Paglia, facing the house of the gondolier, Luigi, and that he is hoping to seduce his with this gift.

THEODORA

(low)

Violetta—so it was he, the unknown man that Maffeo was telling me about—?

BELLAMONTE

And what sort of demon are you?

BRAVO

I am an alchemist from Ferrara in search of the philosopher's and, while waiting to find it, amuses himself to tell good adventures to young cavaliers and young girls.

THEODORA

(going to Bellamonte and taking him by the arm)

Count de Bellamonte, I think that instead of the young Frenchman, instead of plunging into the depths thirty feet—to find that ring—you had better await the death of the Doge—since to marry the sea in a second wedding—would have been more prudent—Let's go to church, and as we are reasonable folks, we will pray for fools.

BELLAMONTE

Let's go, Madame—but I really hope you don't believe a word that this wretched fortune teller said to you.

THEODORA

Oh! We will speak about it again at the party I am giving this evening—I do not hold you quit of the accusation—but let's leave profane things, milords, we are going into Saint Mark's.

(they enter Saint Mark's)

LUIGI

(to Michelemma)

You hear that?

MICHELEMMA

What's that uproar?

(The crowd—behind the stage.)

VOICES

Justice! Justice!

MICHELEMMA

It's some riot among the people—I am going in.

LUIGI

As for me, I'm staying—I will tell you what it's about.

SHOUTS

To the Ducal palace.

BRAVO

What's that?

LUIGI

Ah, it's the young girl and the people coming to demand justice for the murder of an old man—

BRAVO

That's a new thing to be heard: shouting for justice for a murder—in the streets of Venice.

VIOLETTA

Oh! Leave me alone, my friends—my good friends.

SHOUTS

Justice! Justice!

VIOLETTA

Yes, yes—justice I demand it like you. But you scare me. Your shouts are going to overwhelm me. Your shouts frighten me—my God! My God!

A MAN OF THE PEOPLE

No, no, it's necessary that justice be done to the people when the people demand justice—we are bringing you in our arms, we will bring you to the face of the tribunal, unto the feet of the Doge and we will see to it that justice is done to you.

VIOLETTA

You will get me killed, that's all—have pity, have pity!

(she falls to her knees)

BRAVO

(placing his hand on Violetta)

Leave this young girl alone. The caresses of the people are like those of the lion, they suffocate.

(he takes Violetta by the hand)

Come, child—and breathe at your ease.

VIOLETTA

Thanks, thanks! You are my guardian angel.

(she lowers her veil over her face)

BRAVO

(to people)

Well, what do you want, now—? Speak.

A MAN OF THE PEOPLE

They killed old Maffeo—a man of the people who never did anything against the Republic—they killed him in the name of the Republic—it's some private vengeance under this name—they killed him treacherously and we are demanding justice.

BRAVO

And you, what do you want—child?

VIOLETTA

(joining her hands)

As for me, I don't want anything—nothing—just to weep for my father, for he was my father—since I don't have any family! I was at home—everybody came running, all this crowd rushed in carrying a bloody body—it was that of Maffeo! Then, without pity for my shouts, for my tears, they took me, enveloped me, dragged me—without my knowing where we are going—talking of blood and death and demanding justice.

BRAVO

(to people)

And justice against who—?

A MAN OF THE PEOPLE

Against the Bravo.

BRAVO

You are quite bold, you are—and in whose name are you demanding justice—when the nobility, the Senate don't dare ask it—?

A MAN OF THE PEOPLE

We demand it in the name of the people.

BRAVO

And if they refuse it to you?

A MAN OF THE PEOPLE

We will do it ourselves.

BRAVO

The time hasn't come and the wind is blowing away your words.

(to Violetta)

And you, young girl—do you want justice, too? Do you also want the death of the Bravo?

VIOLETTA

I want a convent where I can serve God—a cell where I can weep.

BRAVO

(aside)

Weep! Weep! Poor child—why did I meet you on my path—! Oh! In saving you from Bellamonte, perhaps I will repair some of the evil I have done you.

(aloud)

Yes, to you—there must be a convent, a cell—for you are an angel. You are too beautiful and too pure for the world of men.

A MAN OF THE PEOPLE

But still, it's necessary that someone greet the orphan—and if no one presents himself—the Doge must serve as her father and Venice as her mother—

BRAVO

The Doge is an inflexible father and hard on his children—Venice is a mother debauched and ruined—neither the one nor the other are worthy of such a daughter—child—

VIOLETTA

(raising her head)

Milord!

BRAVO

You have no relative in the world?

VIOLETTA

None.

BRAVO

You don't know anyone in this city?

VIOLETTA

No one—except a woman still young and very beautiful who

comes to see me from time to time—and who seems to love me a lot—but I don't even know her name. Maffeo alone knew this secret and he took it with him—

BRAVO

You desire only a convent and a cell?

VIOLETTA

I only want that.

BRAVO

And you cannot pay your dowry?

VIOLETTA

I don't have any—

BRAVO

You heard, my masters, this child does not desire anything in the world except a convent but she has nothing to pay her dowry with—I will pay it— This child is an orphan, isolated—without support; she has no father—I will serve as one to her—you would like a rich man to adopt her; I am rich and I am adopting her—have you still got something to say?

A MAN OF THE PEOPLE

No, if she accepts.

BRAVO

Do you accept my child?

VIOLETTA

Yes, for no question, heaven sent you to a poor orphan to guard and protect her—

A MAN OF THE PEOPLE

God keep the two of you, then.

BRAVO

(taking Violetta in his arms)

(aside)

Bellamonte, you will have a hard time finding her—

(aloud)

Make way for father and daughter.

PEOPLE

Long live the unknown—! Death to the Bravo! Long live the stranger—the rich Lord! Death to the Bravo—Death!

(At this moment, Salfieri appears all in black his face covered by his black mask, at the top of the stairway of the Giants. The people shut up when they notice him and retreat step for step as he descends the step and separate before him and allow him to calmly take his place at the foot of the Lion column.)

CURTAIN

ACT II
SCENE 4

Theodora's oratory.

Someone knocks at the door. Michelemma goes to open.

MICHELEMMA

It's you, Luigi.

LUIGI

Personally.

MICHELEMMA

And what chance brings you here?

LUIGI

Am I not the confidential gondolier of the Signora?

MICHELEMMA

Well—but—the station of a gondolier is—

LUIGI

In his gondola—logical, very logical—but I said to myself—if I were to profit by the moment in which the Signora Theodora is not here, so as to see this oratory which causes so much talk in Venice, that the Chapel of Saint Ambrose is jealous of it, that I would do better than to remain on the Piazetta which probably at this hour I'd be wearing myself out. Sonofabitch! It deserves its reputation. When I think of the quantity of souls who lose their way passing through here, and who, instead of honestly following the path to paradise have passed through this door which really to me resembles a vestibule of hell—

MICHELEMMA

Silence! The Signora.

THEODORA

(entering)

Who is this man?

MICHELEMMA

The Gondolier that Your Highness is attaching to your service—

THEODORA

Leave.

(to Michelemma and Luigi)

THEODORA

(to Bellamonte who has followed her in)

Decidedly, Count—you are the most obstinate man in Venice—that's a justice that I am delighted to do you.

BELLAMONTE

Say the most amorous, Madame, that's a confession I am pleased to make you.

THEODORA

Then it's sad that this obstinate love or this pig-headed passion, whatever you wish to call your eternal pursuit, comes to clash with a will as inflexible as mine—

God forgive me, I think that if you took it in your head to become a great man, with half as much perseverance you would already be halfway there.

BELLAMONTE

That, Madame, is the affair of my ancestors who very willingly set themselves to making a name for me—

THEODORA

Which you take it upon yourself to unmake; you are of a lucky family—in enterprises, Count.

BELLAMONTE

But Madame, I thought that a noble name was of some importance to you!

THEODORA

When one bears it, yes—when it bears you, no.

BELLAMONTE

The name of Bellamonte is inscribed in the table of marble and the book of gold—and it will remain there so long as Venice is counted among the cities of the world and bears its crown as Queen of the Adriatic.

THEODORA

If Venice is Queen of the Adriatic, I am Queen of Venice—and I, like she, I have my tables of marble and my book of gold—but those will live even when Venice is no longer—cast your eyes on these Frescoes and read—here's the name Michelangelo under a Holy family—that of Raphael written on a stone of the Virgin Mary of the Ruins—that of Saint Cecilia, for which I posed—a signed Julio Romano—this Christ in the tomb, of which I have the original and that God has only the copy of is by Titian those are my tables of marble—

(she opens a book)

Now, sir, this sonnet is by Guicciardini; this strophe is by Ariosto, this maxim by Machiavelli, this little song by Trissino: that's my book of gold—for all these things were written for me by those who made them—I told you that I was queen—this crown is as valuable as that of the Doge, I hope—eh, look, Count Bellamonte, here are empty baskets, here are blank pages—take a pen—take a brush, a decoration the more—

BELLAMONTE

There are men who came into the world to create books and pictures, and others who were born to buy them. Is there a picture in the palace of the Doge which pleases you? I will cover it with sequins. Do you want the original manuscript of Orlando Furioso or Il Principe! Tell me again, I will go find Ariosto or

Machiavelli and I will in exchange barter the clasp on this book, which will make them so rich as to never more be obliged to make the wretched profession of poet to make a living. But a brush stroke, a pen jumping would stain the Escutcheon of a Bellamonte.

THEODORA

Well then, Lord Count, take the word of Trivulce or Doria, pass through your belt the dagger of Fiesque or Rienzi—fight for the Republic or against the Republic. Become a general or a conspirator—instead of Count Bellamonte, call yourself Bellamonte the victorious or Bellamonte the proscribed, come to me with whatever celebrity may be yours and then say to me, "Theodora, I want you!"

(laughing)

You shall have me.

BELLAMONTE

So until then—

THEODORA

Until then, you must content yourself with purchasing chains of gold for young girls who live behind the bridge of Paglia facing the house of the Gondolier Luigi.

BELLAMONTE

Well, Madame, I will follow your advice and with this step, I am going to bring it to her—

(he leaves)

THEODORA

Oh—I will be there before you, Count de Bellamonte and I swear to you, I will find for her a retreat so profound you will never discover it.

Michelemma! Luigi! Michelemma.

MICHELEMMA

(entering)

Signora!

THEODORA

Quick! Quick! Luigi and his gondola.

MICHELEMMA

Luigi.

LUIGI

(entering)

Signora.

THEODORA

Luigi, you are going to take me opposite your place, behind the bridge of Paglia—to the house of old Maffeo.

LUIGI

Then the Signora is going to his burial?

THEODORA

What are you saying?

LUIGI

Maffeo was murdered yesterday.

THEODORA

Maffeo—that old man—and the child—the young girl that was in his home?

LUIGI

The Signora—

THEODORA

Violetta—where is she? What's become of her?

LUIGI

A stranger carried her off this morning.

THEODORA

Look, my God! Explain yourself—all that you are saying to me is crazy—I don't understand a thing—!

LUIGI

Maffeo is dead. The young girl was brought this morning to the public square by the people who demanded justice for the orphan—and she has been adopted by a foreigner no one in Venice knows—and who knows everybody.

THEODORA

And this stranger?

LUIGI

Took her away.

THEODORA

Ah, all this is enough to crack one's head and one's heart. At the hour I was at church and I was praying God all this time! While Maffeo was being killed and Violetta was being carried off! And this happened in the Square, two steps from me—oh! To whom to address myself in Venice to have this child back! My gold, my diamonds, this palace—who will tell me where Violetta is—where my daughter is!

MICHELEMMA and LUIGI

Her daughter!

THEODORA

Yes, my daughter! She's my daughter—I want my daughter—let them return my daughter to me—

LUIGI

There's only one man who could do it, Madame.

THEODORA

Who? Let him be brought to me: I will embrace his knees!

LUIGI

(pointing to the Bravo)

It's the one who is down there, at the foot of the column.

THEODORA

The Bravo?

LUIGI

The Bravo.

THEODORA

Run, Luigi, say that it's a mother—bring him—he will come, he must come; tell him I am rich, go find him, bring him to me. There, there Michelemma, my mantilla, my veil, my mask! Ah—poor child! Poor Violetta! God! There's Luigi, going to him—will speak to him—

(making a sign at the window)

Come—come—he's here, well, he's refusing.

(extending her arms to him)

I beg you.

Oh—I'm going to run to him myself.

MICHELEMMA

Madame! Madame!

You—speak to that man, on the public square, in broad daylight—facing all Venice—impossible—impossible! Give me a word—some lines for him—and I will go find him.

THEODORA

(writing)

"My life, my fortune is yours if you come." Take this letter—take it.

(Michelemma leaves running)

(falling on her knees, running)

My God! Lord! My God!—My God? Oh! Oh! How wretched am I!

(rising and running to the window)

Go, Michelemma—will you go! She's speaking to him—he is asking her if it's I who wrote it—

(opening the blind)

Yes, yes, it's me—me—me—there he is—he's coming. Ah! My God! My God! Here he is!

SALFIERI

(rushing into the apartment)

It's from you—this letter, Madame?

THEODORA

It's from me.

SALFIERI

In your writing?

THEODORA

Yes.

SALFIERI

(aside)

The handwriting on the torn letter forgotten in Geneva.

(aloud)

Speak: What do you want from me?

THEODORA

My daughter!

SALFIERI

You have a daughter? Ah!

THEODORA

I did have one—

SALFIERI

What do you mean?

THEODORA

Oh! A treasure! Nothing like her under heaven! That I hid from all eyes! It's two weeks that I made her come to Venice.

SALFIERI

From Genoa.

THEODORA

Yes—with—

SALFIERI

Maffeo—and she's called—

THEODORA

Violetta.

SALFIERI

Violetta!

THEODORA

Well, Maffeo's been assassinated and Violetta's lost!

SALFIERI

Lost! Lost! Violetta lost! I will find her for you, woman!

THEODORA

So, you see, if you find her for me, whatever you want, my fortune, my blood, my life, a crime, you can ask anything!

SALFIERI

You swear it to me!

THEODORA

Yes, I swear it to you. I am addressing myself to you because you must know everything; a man carried her off this morning—there, in this square—in the face of Venice! You must find this man for me; he is unknown, they tell me—but there is no one unknown to you. He's a foreigner, but no one enters Venice or leaves it without your knowing where he's going or where he comes from.

SALFIERI

Oh! Don't worry; all that can be done, I will do; but also—what I shall ask, you will give me.

THEODORA

Yes—everything, everything, everything—I am making you an oath and this oath, it's a mother who is making it, a mother, meaning what is most sacred on Earth after God! And who makes it to you not by a Madonna, not by a saint, not by Christ—but by the life of her daughter.

SALFIERI

That's fine.

THEODORA

Don't waste a moment! Search Venice like a miser whose treasure was stolen—like a lover whose mistress has been ravished from him. Palaces and hovels, vessels and gondolas, quays and streets—visit all—go, in the name of heaven! Go, go, go! And you won't return without her?

SALFIERI

You will see us together or you will never see either one of us.

(he leaves)

THEODORA

(falling to her knees)

My God! Lord! You, who saw your son die! Give me back my daughter!

CURTAIN

ACT III
SCENE 5

The Bravo.

Same as first act.

BRAVO

(watching Violetta sleep)

Such a sweet and holy thing: A child sleeping, and how marvelous with this angel face from which the hand of Man has not yet effaced the finger of God!

Poor child! Lost and abandoned! Oh! I really must shelter you, I who made you an orphan! God arranges things in this world by means that escape the sight of men—God is great and merciful, for I neither expected nor deserved this joy.

VIOLETTA

(awakening)

Ah! My God!

BRAVO

My child!

VIOLETTA

Where am I? Where have they taken me?

BRAVO

Don't be afraid.

VIOLETTA

(calling)

Maffeo! Maffeo!

BRAVO

Oh! Don't call that old man in that tone; for it seems to me he would emerge form the tomb to answer you.

VIOLETTA

It's true! It's true! Dead—dead—dead!

BRAVO

(aside)

Oh! On the day of the last judgment, how many voices around me will shout: dead—dead—dead!

VIOLETTA

Pardon—oh! I know all that I owe you—you gathered me up, weeping and broken at your feet where I had fallen from lack of support; the hour at which the gates of the Convent of Saint Marie usually are open having passed, you said to me: "Child, until tomorrow you will accept the asylum that your second father is offering to you?" And until tomorrow, I have consented to remain under your protection—because you are good, I am sure of it; but when I woke up like this alone, with an unknown man, as for me, young girl that I am—I trembled.

BRAVO

For your life?

VIOLETTA

Oh! No—

BRAVO

Come child, and look at me. I am barely 35 years old, it is true, but have you seen at my age, many faces as wrinkled as mine, many faces as pale? I am like the trees on the Lido—you see, around which so many storms have scolded, they are dry on their boughs and bear neither flowers nor fruit.

(striking his face)

Nothing more here! Only a sinister, incessant, eternal thought.

(striking his heart)

Nothing more there! Only a bottomless abyss—wherein men have thrown crime and remorse.

VIOLETTA

Crime and remorse—

BRAVO

Yes—and those are two words in a foreign tongue that you do not know—

VIOLETTA

You know them—you—My God!

BRAVO

You will make me forget them—yes, in return for what I have been able to do for you, I will ask only one favor.

VIOLETTA

Speak.

BRAVO

(with a tone of prayer)

You will allow me to come to the convent you have chosen there, seeing you happy and calm, you will hear me tell you that you owe this calm and happiness to me. That's all the share of happiness that I can still hope for in this world—and I will owe it to you, child—will you grant it to me?

VIOLETTA

The poor orphan girl that you gathered up, adopted—could she refuse you that?

BRAVO

Thanks.

VIOLETTA

But—why did you speak to me just now of crimes, of remorse? You, so kind, so generous—oh! Can you have had days in your past whose memory weighs on you?

BRAVO

At the hour of birth, fate writes the history of men on a book of iron—each day time turns the page and man does what is written.

VIOLETTA

Oh! What are you telling me?

BRAVO

And were he virtuous and good, such as you think me, he must obey his destiny—were it to order him to do murder—

VIOLETTA

Oh! Why are you blaspheming, for God has said, "Thou shalt not kill."

BRAVO

God! Keep your belief, child, as for me—I've always doubted.

VIOLETTA

You?

BRAVO

Sine a story was told me that froze my faith—oh, it's a strange story—Violetta—I have a few minutes still to remain with you—let me tell you it—after having heard it, you will understand, perhaps, how skepticism comes to men—will you listen to me?

VIOLETTA

Oh, yes! Speak—

BRAVO

Well, sit down—once upon a time in Venice—I no longer know exactly when—a young man of twenty-six—brave—and who is living happily without the memory of a first crime—

Perhaps that crime was the one God wanted to punish—

This young man had a father that he loved with a holy and filial love—

One day, under the pretext of a conspiracy which he didn't even know about—this young man and his father who were dwelling outside of Venice—were arrested. They were dragged before the Council of Ten and there—iniquitously, and without witness by the power which belongs neither to God nor men—but which the Council of Ten arrogates to himself—the tribunal condemned the old man—and acquitted the young man. They took the old man to prison—they set the young man free. Are you listening, my child?

VIOLETTA

But what did the young man do?

BRAVO

The young man dragged himself to their feet; offered his blood in exchange for the blood of his father, his life to purchase the life of his father—the tribunal—oh! It was derision to make heavenly thunder fall—the Tribunal replied that it was a tribunal of justice—that in its justice it had condemned the father and acquitted the son—that the son would live that the father would die—

VIOLETTA

Oh! That's frightful.

BRAVO

Wait a bit more—wait then, young girl; for I have told you nothing—when he returned home, the son found the President of the Tribunal.

VIOLETTA

Ah!

BRAVO

He, too, was an old man—

VIOLETTA

And he brought the son mercy for his father.

BRAVO

(laughing)

That's it. Listen! The Republic had need of a man sure and devoted—whose arm would be blind and whose dagger—mortal—of a man, who, at all hours of the night, on an order of the Tribunal would execute without hesitation the sentence rendered—it had need in the end of an executioner who killed not only by day—and he was coming to propose to the young man the life of his father—on the condition that he would be this murderer—of whom the Tribunal was in need. It is true that he was allowed to place a mask on his face so as to remain unknown.

VIOLETTA

He refused!

BRAVO

With honor! That night the young man received for the next day permission to see his father.

VIOLETTA

Oh! The Tribunal was softening.

BRAVO

Yes—the next day he ran to find this old man that he no longer hoped to embrace. There was a terrible scene that this father—who blessed—and this son—who blasphemed—

Meanwhile, a town crier stopped beneath the prison window. He read in a loud voice the judgment against the old men—and neither the father nor the son lost a word.

The blessings and the blasphemings ceased—the old man fell back on the floor, and they came to tell the son that it was time to leave. Returning home, he found the President of the Tribunal, who came anew to propose to him the bloody bargain.

VIOLETTA

And again he refused—

BRAVO

Yes, again—the next day, the young man received a new permission to see his father—and he rushed to the prison—they had given to the condemned another cell—this one gave on the Piazetta—the Son and the Father rushed weeping into each other's arms.

Soon there was a great uproar on the plaza; the two unfortunates cast their eyes on the window. In the midst of the square was a block—near this block a man dressed in red who held a long sword in his hand. Then surrounding this block and this man, a whole population waited—they were going to execute the old man.

VIOLETTA

Ah!

BRAVO

That white and venerated head which the son was pressing to his breast—it was going to fall—there—there beneath his eyes—there—there—there.

VIOLETTA

Oh! The son accepted the bargain proposed by the tribunal?

BRAVO

Thanks, young girl, thanks—the son put the mask on his face—a dagger on his belt and went to the Council of Ten—and said, "Here I am!"

BRAVO

And since then?

BRAVO

Since then—the son was sold body and soul. He became the terror and executioner of Venice—but his father lived. Every day he received orders for new murders—but his father lived. He no longer slept at night—no more resting during the day—he no longer believed in anything that was sacred to him before—neither in Providence, nor in God—but each night he had permission to see the old men.

(seven strikes)

Listen.

VIOLETTA

Seven o'clock.

BRAVO

Goodbye, my child, I must leave.

VIOLETTA

Are you leaving me alone like this?

BRAVO

You have nothing to fear—no one will come. Don't open anyway, except to someone who raps like this, three times. It will be me.

(he leaves)

VIOLETTA

(alone)

Oh! Yes. He's right, it's a terrible story and which would be capable of making me doubt everything, if God did not have mysterious ways—! What would become of me if I were alone like that, if I didn't know how to bend my knees before some holy image.

(seeking with her eyes)

Why I am searching in vain—no Madonna—no crucifix in this room—Oh, my God! Little matter to you right? From wherever it parts from—and before any altar wherever it may be, the prayer of the weak always climbs to you! My God! You have taken from me my father and my mother before I was able to know them—a man had replaced them—and you called him back to you. There's only one single being under Heaven for whom I can pray: watch over the life of Salfieri.

(three knocks at the door)

Is this my protector? Already back? Oh, it's impossible—still it's the way he told me he would rap—let's open.

VIOLETTA

Ah—it's not him!

SALFIERI

A young girl here—Violetta.

VIOLETTA

My God! My God—from where do you know my name?

SALFIERI

Violetta, here—near me—Violetta lost and found—ah, despite my oath—Violetta, before you alone I will tear off my mask—

VIOLETTA

Salfieri.

SALFIERI

Yes, Salfieri who is searching for you to return you to your mother.

VIOLETTA

My mother—I have a mother? Me?

SALFIERI

Yes, you, Violetta—eh! Why it's a dream! A delirium. Oh—speak to me—look at me—Violetta—your voice—your eyes—

you haven't forgotten me—?

VIOLETTA

I was praying for you and God heard me—oh! How happy I am now! But why this mask?

SALFIERI

This mask—am I not proscribed in Venice, and lost if I am discovered?

VIOLETTA

Oh!

SALFIERI

What makes me run the danger I am running? Violetta, I've seen you again! And your mother, your mother has found you—do you understand? Your mother, your mother to whom I am going to return you and swore to me, on your life, to grant me what I will ask of her.

VIOLETTA

And what will you ask?

SALFIERI

My happiness and yours—your life and mine.

VIOLETTA

You have then read in the mirror?

SALFIERI

Yes—the word Venice—

VIOLETTA

And you left to follow me?

SALFIERI

On the first vessel that made sail.

VIOLETTA

All proscribed as you were?

SALFIERI

I would have confronted a thousand deaths to reach you—but let's leave—leave—!

VIOLETTA

Leave—oh! How can I without giving thanks to my benefactor, without telling him that I've found my mother. She loves me then, my mother?

SALFIERI

Oh, yes, yes—but you are speaking of what benefactor—

VIOLETTA

The one who lives in this house—it's he who gathered me up—

SALFIERI

What! That man? The Br—

(three knocks at the door)

VIOLETTA

(running to the door)

Here he is!

SALFIERI

Silence, Violetta—go back into that room. Oh—let me alone with him—go in.

VIOLETTA

Oh! My God! Leave you—if by going I lost you again!

SALFIERI

Fear nothing—don't be afraid—I am watching over you now.

(A second rap—Violetta goes into the adjoining room—Salfieri goes to the door and opens it.)

BRAVO

(recoiling)

Malediction! A man here—!

SALFIERI

Eh! What's so astonishing when that man is me?

BRAVO

It's true I had forgotten that you knew how to make the door open—but where is the young girl?

SALFIERI

She is there.

BRAVO

(hand on his dagger)

Did you tell her who I am?

SALFIERI

If she knew you would she still be here?

BRAVO

Fine. Now what do you want?

SALFIERI

Now—I want that young girl who is here.

BRAVO

What's this you are saying, wretch?

SALFIERI

Listen—if I had wanted to carry her off in your absence I could do it—but that would have been a bad payment for your confidence—and your hospitality—I awaited your return.

BRAVO

Hoping that I would grant you this insane demand.

SALFIERI

Hoping.

BRAVO

You are mistaken. This young girl is mine. I won't give her up to anyone.

SALFIERI

Not even to her mother?

BRAVO

What are you saying? To her mother! She doesn't have one.

SALFIERI

She does have one, and I left her—and I am coming in her name to demand her of you—I didn't know she was here—I was rushing to say to you, "Help me!"—you who know everything that happens in Venice, help me to return a girl to her mother. I found this child here—she told me about the death of Maffeo—she told me you had adopted her—and then I recognized that she was the one I was seeking—

BRAVO

And you are asking for her in the name of her mother?

SALFIERI

In the name of a mother in tears, who dragged herself at my feet shouting "Mercy from God."

BRAVO

That's really sacred—a mother—

SALFIERI

Yes, yes—it's sacred—a mother has rights over her child that no one can ravish from her but God—this one especially seems to love her daughter so much.

BRAVO

And who is she—where does she live?

SALFIERI

In the palace which is on the corner of the Piazetta, facing the Lion Column.

BRAVO

Why that's the palace of Theodora.

SALFIERI

Yes, that's it—that's it—that name is indeed the one to be found at the bottom of the letter she wrote me. Her mother's named

Theodora.

BRAVO

She wants her daughter returned to her?

SALFIERI

She demands it on her knees—

BRAVO

Ah, this no longer astonishes me. Theodora is asking for her daughter back—the courtesan wants her pupil—it's necessary that she link to Venice an heir that will replace her—in fame and infamy—

SALFIERI

What are you saying?

BRAVO

And you undertook to take such a pure child to a mother as ruined the way she is?

SALFIERI

But, as for me, I know nothing of all this.

BRAVO

You don't know that there are two reputations in Venice of which one can balance the other—the one is that of the courtesan and the other that of the Bravo.

SALFIERI

My God!

BRAVO

Ah! Theodora—lost soul—damned soul—ah, you want your daughter to drag her with you into the abyss, you want this angel so as to snatch anyway her halo, to plunge her into your hell! And when God, in a moment of pity for such a sweet and beautiful creature—instead of blessing God—just once—you ask that she be brought back to you! Didn't she ask that, as you told me—?

SALFIERI

Yes.

BRAVO

Well, that's fine—I will take her to her myself.

SALFIERI

It wasn't to you but to me that she said—

BRAVO

She told you to find her daughter—go tell her that she's been found—go tell her that before tomorrow morning she'll be brought to her—and that if this child wants to remain here no one will oppose her.

SALFIERI

But if, against all probability this child doesn't wish to remain with her mother—what will become of her?

BRAVO

There are three hundred monasteries in Venice—she will chose the one she wishes and I will pay it a Queen's dowry.

SALFIERI

And if I don't adopt all these plans—if I want to have her back immediately—for this young girl—she's Violetta—Violetta whom I love and was seeking.

BRAVO

To make her into your mistress, right? For the noble Salfieri would he give his name to the daughter of a courtesan?

SALFIERI

After her mother, I alone have rights over this child, and if I intend to turn them to account—

BRAVO

Then I will say to you what yesterday you said to me at a similar hour—there are two of us—both young—both strong, both brave, I think—and each of us has a dagger at his belt. Listen, I trust, you trust me—I have offered you may hand—offer me yours.

SALFIERI

Above all, I will be able when I wish it to consult about her wishes with this child.

BRAVO

Very fine—

SALFIERI

And the will of this child will be followed.

BRAVO

In every respect.

SALFIERI

Here's my hand.

BRAVO

Now, go back to Theodora. Isn't she giving a party tonight?

SALFIERI

Yes—but the loss of her daughter—

BRAVO

Well, go tell her that she can give her party—for her daughter has been found.

SALFIERI

I have confidence in you—but think—

BRAVO

Yesterday, when you presented yourself here at this very hour—

you told me that with a word, I could kill you—well! In my turn, one word could be mortal to me—if I deceive you—take the Council of Ten this mask and this dagger—accuse me of having left them for an hour—and all will be said.

SALFIERI

That's fine.

BRAVO

Goodbye!

SALFIERI

Goodbye!

(he leaves)

BRAVO

(opening Violetta's door)

Come my child.

VIOLETTA

(emerging)

Where is he?

BRAVO

That young man?

VIOLETTA

The one who came to find me in the name of my mother.

BRAVO

He left—

VIOLETTA

And everything is agreed with him?

BRAVO

All.

VIOLETTA

And he will bring me back to my mother?

BRAVO

It will be I who escorts you to her.

VIOLETTA

Oh! You are right; it's from you that she ought to receive me.

BRAVO

Put on your veil and your mantilla—my child.

(he presents the mantilla to her)

VIOLETTA

(placing it on her shoulders)

Then we are going now?

BRAVO

To find a costume for the ball for you.

VIOLETTA

For the ball?

BRAVO

(slowly)

Yes—we will go—tonight to a masked ball.

CURTAIN

ACT IV
SCENE 6

The Palace of Theodora—whole rooms resplendent with light. Fantastical architecture. A combination of three styles, Greek, Gothic, Moorish. Masks of all sorts.

The Marquis de Ruffo—the Count de Bellamonte—Michelemma—young lords—two masked women who seem to avoid the pursuit of the Marquis de Ruffo emerge from the crowd.

FIRST WOMAN

There he is again.

SECOND WOMAN

For the last time, Milord, I forbid you to follow us thus.

RUFFO

(aside)

No doubt at all.

(aloud)

I had need to hear your voice, my pretty Venetian—now press your mask as carefully to your face—little matter to me—I know you.

FIRST WOMAN

Oh! My God.

RUFFO

And you, too—for one of you wears a ring that yesterday I also saw on the finger of the charming wife of Providiter Ordenego—the other—

FIRST WOMAN

Oh! Mercy! Milord, don't name me here.

RUFFO

(lowering his voice)

Is it with the permission of the grave Senator Zeno you are here, Madame?

FIRST WOMAN

Oh, speak lower! And on your honor promise us the secret for a week. It's been noised about in Venice about the brilliant party of Theodora.

By means of this disguise, by the shadow of this mask, we wanted to see this palace of the new Armida, we wanted to be present at her enchantments. You have recognized us, Marquis—with a word you could ruin us—but you won't utter that word.

RUFFO

I'll shut up—although it costs me—but you will permit me to be for the entire night—your cavalier servant.

FIRST WOMAN

Oh—it's unnecessary—a few minutes more and we are leaving—don't make us noticed.

RUFFO

You wish it, I obey—goodbye, Madame, count on my discretion.

FIRST WOMAN

Count on our gratitude.

(they lose themselves in the crowd)

RUFFO

(watching the move away)

Noble prudes, there's a secret I will make you pay dearly for—! Ah! Michelemma, Michelemma.

MICHELEMMA

Milord.

RUFFO

Do you still have orders to flee me?

MICHELEMMA

Do you still have the courage to speak to me?

RUFFO

Will you tell me from what Sabbath you brought the sorcerer to whom you gave your arm?

MICHELEMMA

I don't know any more than you—

BELLAMONTE

Michelemma.

MICHELEMMA

Milord.

BELLAMONTE

Is your mistress in the habit of not appearing at the balls she gives?

MICHELEMMA

Do you have the habit of coming to balls to which you are not invited?

BELLAMONTE

But all that Venice has of young folks of style and nobility are invited here by right.

RUFFO

(approaching)

From the replies, Chamberlaine, one can guess that the affairs of Count Bellamonte are favoring ill with the mistress.

BELLAMONTE

And that's a misfortune for which the Marquis de Ruffo ought to experience a great sympathy—

(Bravo enters with face uncovered. Violetta is veiled—they arrive behind Bellamonte and Ruffo and stop, listening to their conversation.)

RUFFO

Also, I was seeking you that we might consult together.

BELLAMONTE

Let's concern ourselves with you, Marquis—with me it's a matter that's done.

RUFFO

You are very lucky, Count; as for me, I admit, that it costs me to give up hope of being loved by Theodora.

BELLAMONTE

Well! We will make an exception. It's always honorable in a time of generalities.

RUFFO

When I think that wretched scoundrels of poets and painters, have known how to please this woman.

BELLAMONTE

That's what has disgusted people of nobility and family with her—

VIOLETTA

(in a half voice)

Oh! My God! Of what woman are they speaking like this?

BRAVO

Believe me that I would not have done it, my child, without an imperative motive—

RUFFO

Bellamonte! See there that man alone without a mask in the midst of us?

BELLAMONTE

(looking)

Here!

RUFFO

You know him?

BELLAMONTE

That is to say that he knows me, as for me, I would die the death of a villain if, before this morning I had ever seen his face—but after what he said to me, I have to believe him to be a sorcerer or a demon—

RUFFO

He's bringing with him a companion of gracious shape.

VIOLETTA

(frightened)

Those masks are looking at us.

BRAVO

Don't be afraid of anything, they won't come to speak to us.

VIOLETTA

Never mind, let's move to another room, I beg you.

(Great uproar at the back. The masks are agitated—the name Theodora can be heard to circulate, she appears surrounded by several young men—all masked.)

BELLAMONTE

(striding to meet her)

Ah, Madame, you are like the star of Venice—which rises last and most beautiful.

THEODORA

Ah, it's you, Count—without animosity—I am so happy this evening that I want everyone to be happy.

RUFFO

You told Bellamonte—without rancor—will you tell me again without hope?

THEODORA

It's you, Marquis—hope is one of the theological virtues—keep it, as I keep its sister—charity.

RUFFO

I lack faith.

THEODORA

(giving him her hand)

I give it to you—

RUFFO

(kissing her hand)

Oh! Madame—

BELLAMONTE

It's only I who will remain unhappy.

THEODORA

You, Count—O! Dangerous as you are, you would be the last of men that I would want to lose

COUNT

I will await my turn.

THEODORA

(seeing the Bravo)

Huh! But what's this lord coming to my place with his face unmasked.

BELLAMONTE

You who know all of Venice—will you extricate us from our embarrassment, Madame, and tell us who he is?

THEODORA

I don't know him—Your Lordship has done us the honor of coming to our ball—and we thank you.

BRAVO

Without being invited.

THEODORA

We doubly thank you for coming in that case—and you bring us a compatriot?

BRAVO

Who's coming from the country of Lais to see Aspasia.

THEODORA

Why it's a rival that you are denouncing to us.

BRAVO

No, she's a student who has need of experience and advice and who is coming to demand illumination from the Sun.

THEODORA

I regret that we don't have before her the two Cypriot dancers to execute the dance known as Pyrrhique, and which will remind her of her country but we've brought from Spain, from Seville in Andalousia two marvelous creatures, who dance, they say, the bolero ravishingly—the dance of lust—

VIOLETTA

What language! My God and where am I?

BRAVO

Shut up—

THEODORA

Hey, my gypsies—we are folks of pleasure and love like you. We have a warm sun like yours which makes our heads ardent and our hearts fiery—come on—Your Adalousian dancers who perform the Teutonic Waltz, the Polish mazurka, and the Neapolitan Tarantela.

(Everyone arranges a circle; the Spanish dancers execute the Bolero amidst shouts and bravos from the young lords; Violetta hides her head on the breast of the Bravo.)

BRAVO

Why don't you tell this timid child to watch this dance; tell her that if she wants to follow in your footsteps, she must accustom herself to very candid looks—

THEODORA

Come on, my beautiful Athenian with naked feet—will you watch this dance?

VIOLETTA

In that case, give me your mask, Madame, for soon my veil won't suffice to hide my blushing.

BRAVO

I told you that we were coming to seek lessons, and you've begun with examples—let the voice repair the sin of the eyes—Aspasia preached the art that she practiced—the gardens of Academus were less rich and less resplendent than yours—come on, Aspasia, come on—Alcibiades, Pericles are listening to you—and Socrates is, I hope, refused admittance.

BELLAMONTE

Theodora! Theodora! You hear—

RUFFO

It's a challenge, Madame.

THEODORA

That I accept, gentlemen—

ALL

Come on! Come on, Aspasia.

THEODORA

Aspasia can only speak in the tongue of Sappho—Michelemma, my harp—

STROPHES

O my faithful harp, cease to be mute! I need your tones to support my voice as if pleasure flowered on its wing. When the chord awakes, and sings beneath my fingers.

Pouring ardent, frenzied lust
On hearts where it delights are as yet unknown
Listen Greeks, Its Aspasia
Who's singing of love and Venus.
Not at all youthful love with long timid glances
That dare not raise their eyes to the beloved
And which allow Old Man Time, somber and rapid
To ravish the most joyous of its days unfulfilled
But fickle Cupid with flickering flowers
Butterflies for whom women are flowers—
Which do not alter the colors of next day's tears
Not this Venus, standing ancient and pure
To whom the Lacadaemonians erected alters
Modest deity whose hair
Veiled her divine body from mortal regards—
But that other Venus, disheveled goddess
That Amathonte and Paphos celebrate in chorus

Mistress of Adonis that day in the valley
Mistress of Phoebus by night on the depths of the waves.
Child here's what god, here's what the goddess
Ought to share with our incense and our verse
Of their cult with me, I consecrate you priestess
And to initiate you our temples are open.
Choose according to your taste, leave at your whim
Achilles for Hector, Menelaus for Paris
There's the lesson that Aspasia
Gives to her rival Lais.

BRAVO

Have you nothing more to say?

THEODORA

Nothing, I've finished.

BRAVO

Demon of the abyss! Have you cast your nets—so that this white and candid soul cannot escape you?

THEODORA

All—

BRAVO

Then it's time the lesson be finished. God will make it bear its fruits, I hope—Violetta—

(tearing Theodora's mask off)

There's your mother, Theodora

(raising Violetta's veil)

There's your daughter!

THEODORA

Great God!

VIOLETTA

My mother—you!

BRAVO

Yes—she who reclaims you, my child.

VIOLETTA

Oh—no, no—it's impossible.

BRAVO

Tell her why don't you—that you are her mother—you see plainly she doesn't believe it.

BELLAMONTE

The young girl from the bridge of La Paglia—by Jove, here she will be less cruel, I hope—

RUFFO

She's truly marvelous—and where were you hiding this diamond from us, Theodora?

THEODORA

My God! My God—

BELLAMONTE

Now, young girl—now you have received your lesson—

THEODORA

(with expression)

Gentlemen! Let not one of you soil this child by word or by glance—this child is my daughter—it's true—yes, I am your mother.

VIOLETTA

Ah!

THEODORA

Gentlemen, in the name of your mother and your sisters, respect this child.

BELLAMONTE

You all hear her—respect the daughter of Theodora.

(each laughs)

THEODORA

(throwing herself on Violetta)

Violetta—my child—my daughter—oh—come, here—come

here—it's the heart of a mother—come into my arms and if these young insolents dare to pursue you.

BELLAMONTE

Look—enough, enough. Theodora, everybody's getting sad. The music is stopping—the lights themselves seem to wave—come on, tell the music to play, the dancers to leap.

Take the Marquis de Ruffo's hand and leave me that of your daughter.

THEODORA

(rising)

Count de Bellamonte, I pray you, supplicate you, ask you—mercy—God would have pardoned me in your place and you don't pardon me—you continue to insult a woman who's weeping—Count de Bellamonte, I would give my life, my eternity, everything except my daughter—to be a man—because then I would throw this mask in your face as I am doing.

BELLAMONTE

Madame—

THEODORA

Leave, Milords—everybody leave—for some I entreat you—for the others I order, there's no more ball or party here—leave a mother alone to weep with her daughter—a daughter with her mother.

BELLAMONTE

(laugh)

Marquis, a word.

(he whispers to Ruffo and seems to plan something with him)

BRAVO

Violetta—there's your mother, here's your protector. Stay with her. Come with me—decide.

THEODORA

Oh! You see plainly she is dying—leave her with me, leave her with me. If only until tomorrow, and tomorrow if she wants to leave me, well, you will take her away—but tomorrow, tomorrow my child will love me.

BRAVO

Leave her here! In the midst of these infamous!

THEODORA

Are they still here? Milord, what are you doing here now?

BELLAMONTE

(laughing)

We are organizing the Quadrille of Violetta.

THEODORA

Enough, Bellamonte enough. Gentlemen, I begged you to leave and you haven't done it—I order you to do it—leave and you leave first, count—you are in my home—

BELLAMONTE

We are at your place, Theodora! We are in an elegant hotel where every traveler is well received when he pays. We are at your place, Theodora.

(tossing a purse in the air)

Do like me, gentlemen, we are at home here.

RUFFO

Bellamonte's right—we're at home here—

THEODORA

Oh! My God—my God—that's just too many outrages—

(low)

Violetta, my daughter, stay by this door—we are going to leave this palace.

BRAVO

Where do you intend to take this child?

THEODORA

(low)

To the house of Maffeo—you will serve as our guide—but first—

BRAVO

What are you going to do—?

BELLAMONTE and RUFFO

Come on, Theodora, the signal for the dance.

THEODORA

I am going to give it. You asked just now for the most gay airs—the orchestra is going to obey you—the maddest dancers—begin them—you want to brightest lights—you are going to have a royal illumination—make way!

(She goes to one of the rooms, sets it on fire and returns throwing her torch into another room—yells of terror.)

BELLAMONTE

What have you done?

THEODORA

Nothing. I relit the lights that were beginning to extinguish.

SCREAMS

Fire—fire—

THEODORA

No, stay, Milords—you are at home—

CURTAIN

ACT IV
SCENE 7

A room in Maffeo's house.

Theodora is on her knees before a prieu-dieu simply dressed in brown. Michelemma enters.

MICHELEMMA

Madame—Madame.

THEODORA

Ah! It's you—

MICHELEMMA

Here's the box you asked of me—

THEODORA

Open it, Dear Michelemma—and take among the jewels those you wish—the least precious will suffice to assure you of a happy life.

MICHELEMMA

You are leaving me, then, Madame?

THEODORA

I am leaving everything, Michelemma.

MICHELEMMA

But this rich and happy life—

THEODORA

I curse it.

MICHELEMMA

This world that adores you?

THEODORA

It has ruined me.

MICHELEMMA

These jewels, these diamonds, these necklaces—which make the heart of a woman proud.

THEODORA

Are the chains which link my heart to hell—I am breaking them.

MICHELEMMA

Your palace on the Piazetta?

THEODORA

Was in flames, yesterday—in ruins today. I began it—the people finished it.

MICHELEMMA

The people!

THEODORA

Yes, the people—a strange lion which roars against its master because without doubt one day it's counting on devouring it.

MICHELEMMA

Eh! What will remain to you then?

THEODORA

In this world: Penitence—in the other, hope—my daughter and God.

MICHELEMMA

But me—me, Madame?

THEODORA

Tomorrow Luigi and you, you will be free. You love each other.

MICHELEMMA

Madame.

THEODORA

Leave me alone, Michelemma.

(Michelemma leaves; Violetta enters.)

VIOLETTA

Mother!

THEODORA

(rising)

You called me your mother, right?

VIOLETTA

Yes, I called you my mother, it's a sacred title that the hand of god engraves in the heart and that the hand of man cannot efface.

THEODORA

Thanks—

VIOLETTA

And then, they slandered you—those men—right—?

THEODORA

No, my child—no, those men spoke the truth—and I can admit it, for it's the woman of today who is speaking of the woman of yesterday—for in seeing myself in my daughter—pure and sacred, mirror—I yesterday stripped away the vices of my heart, as today the ornaments of my body—

Yes, for you and through you—I have left everything my child, pleasure and vanity—as rich and brilliant as I was, I am making myself poor and humble—for you and by you, I've said goodbye to the world—and that goodbye I said with a flaming torch in hand—by braving the most powerful of the Venetian aristocracy.

In the end, I trampled underfoot, then passed over that what is worthless and belongs to the demon—I have extended my arms to the future which is mine and God's.

VIOLETTA

In this future you've forgotten me, mother—Am I then nothing to your happiness?

THEODORA

You can forgive me—and then rich in your forgiveness—I can ask of it heaven!

VIOLETTA

O my God! You who see this strange spectacle of a mother at the feet of her daughter—my God, receive in your breast the tears of one and the prayers of the other—and since she says she has need of my pardon and yours—pardon her, my God—as I pardon her.

THEODORA

(on her knees again)

My daughter!

VIOLETTA

(extending her arms to her)

Oh! In your arms—in your arms, my mother!

MICHELEMMA

(entering)

Madame, the stranger of yesterday is here—

THEODORA

He's coming to take you back—

VIOLETTA

Never—never! Mother, let him see us like this and let him dare to separate as—

THEODORA

(holding her in her arms)

Tell him he can come in, Michelemma, let him come in—

(Michelemma exits and the Bravo enters.)

THEODORA

See!

BRAVO

Did you tell her who you are?

THEODORA

I've told her.

BRAVO

You've hidden nothing of your life from her!

THEODORA

Nothing.

BRAVO

And she consents to remain with you?

THEODORA

Ask her!

BRAVO

My child, your will is as free as a bird in the air—you can go where you wish.

VIOLETTA

Where my mother goes—I will go.

BRAVO

Here's an order of the Council which authorizes you despite the wishes of your mother, to enter some convent that you are pleased to choose—a second time, my child, this order in hand, you are free.

VIOLETTA

(giving the order to Theodora)

Here, mother.

THEODORA

You see—you see—I have not said a word—and her heart alone has spoken.

BRAVO

(with a sigh)

That's fine.

THEODORA

I've kept my word—it's up to you to keep yours—you promised me to leave me my child if my child wanted to stay with me. Don't abuse this order that you have got from the Council.

BRAVO

Yes, but now a last question and think that the reply will require a proof. Is Violetta really your daughter?

THEODORA

He asks that. He's seen my despair and my joy—he's seen our embracings—and he asks me if you are my daughter—Oh! Wretch! Did she ask me if I were her mother?

BRAVO

Youth is credulous and full of illusions—ripe age, disenchanted, and difficult to persuade—the proof that Violetta is your daughter—let's see.

THEODORA

Proof—Maffeo alone could give—not the proof but witness—and Maffeo is dead.

BRAVO

I know it.

THEODORA

Maffeo could say she was my daughter—for he picked me up bloody and lifeless.

VIOLETTA

Oh, my mother, and what event?

THEODORA

Oh! That was a terrible drama that began sixteen years ago that began with a murder and ended with an assassination.

BRAVO

(looking at her)

Please God that both were not committed by the same hand—

VIOLETTA

Oh! My mother! And who was the man who dared—

THEODORA

Silence! Silence! Child, it was your father.

VIOLETTA

My father?

THEODORA

He had placed all his hope, all his fortune in me—he thought that I had cheated on him—on your soul, my daughter, it was not true.

BRAVO

Violetta wasn't guilty?

THEODORA

How did you know that my name was Violetta?

BRAVO

Continue—what's it to you from where I know it?

THEODORA

He was a young man—ardent and impetuous—

BRAVO

That Giovanni, right?

THEODORA

Why, how do you know his name was Giovanni?

BRAVO

Continue—continue—

THEODORA

It was during a stormy night, a terrible night, he came in with a storm in his heart more terrible than the storm in heaven—when I saw him go pale, distracted, a dagger in his hand I became so shocked that I couldn't say a word—I didn't try to enlighten him, to convince him—I fell at his feet screaming, "Mercy! Mercy for my child!"

VIOLETTA

And then!

BRAVO

Then I thought she was guilty and I stabbed her—that's all.

THEODORA

Giovanni!

BRAVO

Violetta!

THEODORA

(with soul)

Giovanni, I was innocent and here is your daughter.

BRAVO

My daughter.

VIOLETTA

Oh! My mother—my father—names so delightful to say—my mother! My father—!

BOTH

My child!

VIOLETTA

Now we are reunited—nothing can separate us again—right?

BRAVO and THEODORA

Oh! No, no—nothing.

(A knocking on the door; the three persons on stage shudder.)

BRAVO

There's only one man who can rap like that.

THEODORA

It's him!

(A second knocking.)

BRAVO

It's him!

THEODORA

Giovanni, this man has something to say to me alone.

BRAVO

Still, it's necessary for me to hear what he says to you.

THEODORA

Violetta, go into that room—and you, Giovanni—hide yourself behind the door.

(She goes to open the door; Salfieri appears.)

THEODORA

Come in.

SALFIERI

Theodora, here I am—

THEODORA

I was expecting you.

SALFIERI

Have I faithfully fulfilled on my part all the conditions of our bargain?

THEODORA

All.

SALFIERI

Your daughter was brought to you?

THEODORA

Yes—

SALFIERI

Was she brought to you, safe and pure, as when she was taken from you?

THEODORA

Yes.

SALFIERI

Was that indeed all you asked of me, and not anything else?

THEODORA

That was all.

SALFIERI

Now you recall the oath you took to me—

THEODORA

I swore to you by my daughter to give you anything that you would ask of me if you brought me back—my daughter.

SALFIERI

Are you disposed to do it?

THEODORA

This gold, these jewels are yours—say the word.

SALFIERI

I want a blessing which is more precious to me than all your wealth—

THEODORA

Oh! You make me tremble—what is it you want then?

SALFIERI

I want your daughter—

THEODORA

My Violetta—found yesterday—you want her today—you are mad.

SALFIERI

I want your daughter.

THEODORA

But you see plainly that you can ask any other thing of me—that I've offered you everything—that I will give you everything.

SALFIERI

You swore to me on your daughter to give me whatever I might demand of you—Theodora, I am demanding your daughter.

THEODORA

Oh! My God! But at last—I beg you—if I drag myself at your feet, if I embrace your knees—wouldn't you have pity on a mother—oh, my daughter, my daughter—she's costing me dearly enough for you to leave me with her.

SALFIERI

Meaning that I kept my word and you are reneging on yours.

THEODORA

Listen—you have a dagger in your belt, kill me—and take my daughter afterwards, if you wish—but for me to give her to you—never! Never!

SALFIERI

Theodora—

THEODORA

Why, your idea is senseless—! To believe that a woman can love you—for if you take her, it's to make her your wife or your mistress—she, all pure—you, all bloody—she, Violetta—you, the Bravo—

SALFIERI

And if I wasn't?

BRAVO

(emerging and placing his hand on Giovanna's shoulder)

It's not midnight, my master—and to have the right to demand the word of others, you must begin by keeping yours—

(Meanwhile Theodora has placed herself before her daughter's door.)

THEODORA

What do I hear—he knows this man?

SALFIERI

You're right—but time is slow today.

BRAVO

Perhaps you will find when midnight arrives that the day has passed very quickly—

SALFIERI

Well! So be it—at midnight we will see each other again—but from here on, Theodora, swear to me—

BRAVO

Nothing—no oaths.

SALFIERI

Theodora, I am giving you until midnight—but at midnight you will see me again and then no one will say to me, "Do you want gold, diamonds, palaces?" There'll be no prayers, there'll be no tears—there will be a perjury and heaven will destroy me if I leave to God to punish it—

(Salfieri leaves)

THEODORA

Oh my God! My God! We are lost.

BRAVO

Not yet—Theodora—all your gold is necessary.

THEODORA

Here it is.

BRAVO

Your jewels.

THEODORA

Take them—

BRAVO

Now—all that I possess join to this.

THEODORA

Why—what to do?

BRAVO

A jailor corrupted yesterday that I can seduce today.

THEODORA

A jailor—

BRAVO

Yes—order Luigi to prepare your gondola—

THEODORA

In five minutes it will be moored at the vestibule.

BRAVO

And as for me, in an hour I will be here—

THEODORA

O Giovanni—Giovanni—save my daughter.

CURTAIN

ACT V
SCENE 8

A vestibule giving on the Grand Canal to the left, three-quarters the way back, the door of Theodora—on the same side a marble step supports a lamp and an hourglass—close to the audience—at the right a stone bench. Full night.

Giovanni is leaning against a column which gives on the canal.

THEODORA

(opening the inside door)

Giovanni—Giovanni. What are you waiting for, there?

GIOVIANNI

Luigi.

THEODORA

But come stay with us—and when Luigi gets here he will inform us.

GIOVIANNI

No, no, it's necessary that I make certain without losing a

minute—for I don't have a moment to lose—

I must be certain that he has faithfully followed all my instructions for I indicated to him the place where he must wait for me, as soon as I am sure of being able to find him there—and then we will leave right away.

THEODORA

And where will we go?

GIOVIANNI

I don't know. To the end of the world if need be—you must be as desirous as I am of leaving Venice—Venice whose stay moreover is no longer without danger for you.

THEODORA

Why did you insist that Luigi bring a gondola large enough for five passengers when we are only three?

GIOVIANNI

Theodora, I must bring with me the rings of the chain that binds me to Venice.

THEODORA

Will you keep responding to me in this mysterious language that I cannot understand? You are hiding some horrible secret from me.

GIOVIANNI

Go, stay with your daughter, Theodora, with our daughter—

and tell her to tell you the story I told her—that of the Bravo of Venice.

THEODORA

Oh—since you just mentioned that name of Bravo—let me ask you what you have in common with that execrable man.

GIOVIANNI

Me, me!

THEODORA

And are you under the weight of some proscription?

GIOVIANNI

Get back in, Theodora—

THEODORA

I don't know why—it seems to me I am enchained here—and that I will never leave Venice—Venice, the cursed city—

GIOVIANNI

Soon eleven o'clock—get back inside, I beg you and be ready to leave when I give you the signal—for a moment of delay could ruin us all.

THEODORA

Don't worry—we will be ready—

GIOVIANNI

(pushing her)

That's fine, that's fine.

(she goes in)

(he goes to the back of the stage)

Now—will the jailor be faithful to his promise? It's true that with what I will give him his fortune will be made—and that I will take him with us—oh, so long as in that long procession of corridors I can reach him without being seen—without being heard—right up to the cell of my father—to enter and leave without one door squeaking, without one bolt creaking—it will be a miracle from Heaven—my God! Give pity to that man and strength to me.

But Violetta, but Salfieri, these young folks that love each other and that I am going to separate—oh! Salfieri, he will still love her, the poor child—if he knew her to be the daughter of Theodora, the Courtesan and Giovianni, the Bravo—no—he might still deign to make her his mistress, perhaps—but his wife—at last, Luigi—

(Going to Luigi.)

GIOVIANNI

Is everything ready?

LUIGI

Yes, Excellency.

GIOVIANNI

The gondola can hold—

LUIGI

Seven persons—

GIOVIANNI

That's it—no noise and especially no light; extinguish the lantern.

LUIGI

And the police fine.

GIOVIANNI

I will pay it—that's fine—now don't budge from this spot—think that I will find you again and that at my first sign—

LUIGI

Don't worry, excellency.

GIOVIANNI

Let's go, my God! Protect us.

(Giovanni exits.)

LUIGI

(alone)

All the same, it's a good precaution to have put out the lantern—that made the gondola which followed me after I left my place probably lose my trace—for it really was me that it had the air of being after—but reaching the corner of the canal I made a certain maneuvers which has led my spy astray—so that now I am quite sure.

(One notices the gondola that followed Luigi is landing and putting a man ashore as Luigi goes to knock on the door of Theodora.)

THEODORA

Michelemma! Michelemma!

MICHELEMMA

(on the other side of the door)

Well!

LUIGI

It's me, here I am—tell your mistress that I have arrived and not to worry—

MICHELEMMA

That's fine, stay at your post and don't breathe a word.

LUIGI

Oh! There's no danger of my leaving here, nor of telling anyone for whom this boat is—I'd sooner be cut to pieces.

(turning and noticing the gondola of Salfieri)

Ah!

SALFIERI

Luigi.

LUIGI

The Bravo.

SALFIERI

That boat is for the Signora Theodora?

LUIGI

Yes, Milord.

SALFIERI

The Signora must leave Venice with her daughter?

LUIGI

Yes, Milord.

SALFIERI

Before midnight?

LUIGI

Yes, Milord.

SALFIERI

And you are the discreet gondolier who must guide her through the lagoons?

LUIGI

Yes, Milord.

SALFIERI

That's fine, I'll take charge of your work.

LUIGI

And me, Milord?

SALFIERI

You—you are going to get in this gondola—which you will pilot back to your house and you won't leave there until after midnight.

LUIGI

Yes, Milord.

SALFIERI

You understand?

LUIGI

Perfectly, Milord.

(Gets in his gondola and moves away.)

SALFIERI

(watching Luigi disappear)

Fine—and if now they escape me, either Satan or this man is opening a new path for them.

BAILIFF

(entering and looking all around then advancing on Salfieri, who still wears the costume of the Bravo)

Ah! Finally found you, my master.

SALFIERI

Who is this man?

BAILIFF

The orders of the tribunal that they nail to your door now run a great risk of falling into dust for you no longer return home—

SALFIERI

Explain yourself—what do you want with me?

BAILIFF

You have two hours to obey the Council.

(delivering to him a sealed parchment and withdrawing)

SALFIERI

(alone)

An order of the Council—an order of murder to me—what would have become of me if I'd gotten this order yesterday? Eleven thirty—God be praised—I have two hours to execute the order of the Council and in a half hour I will be free—in a half hour, the mask, the dagger, the murder go to the assassin—to me Violetta, love, liberty, life! Life, happy and peaceful, far from Venice. This Queen with a bloody cloak, this unnatural mother that devours its children—that door is opening—to our post.

MICHELEMMA

(leaving furtively)

No one, Madame, no one except Luigi—for his gondola is moored.

VIOLETTA

Oh, mother—mercy—let's take the air for a moment under this vestibule for the evening is hot—and it's suffocating in this apartment.

THEODORA

It's a very strange story that you've told me.

VIOLETTA

And the hero of that story is a very unhappy man—

THEODORA

Yes—but that's the way things are done in Venice, child—cursed city, city of pleasure, of tears, of blood—oh! Rejoice, my daughter, we are going to leave it—

VIOLETTA

Never to return, mother—

THEODORA

Oh! Never, never—

VIOLETTA

My God—

THEODORA

Regrets—tears—but your father and I will accompany you, child—what can make you weep, what can you make you regret leaving Venice?

VIOLETTA

Oh, mother—the one I was crying over, the one I regretted when I left Genoa—

THEODORA

That young man of whom Maffeo spoke to me and whom I feared you would love—when I recalled you to me—but he's in Genoa—

VIOLETTA

He's in Venice, mother—

THEODORA

And you've seen him again?

VIOLETTA

Yesterday.

THEODORA

Imprudent child that you are, to have given your heart like that—because you love him—

VIOLETTA

Oh! Yes—

THEODORA

To a man who perhaps doesn't love you—

VIOLETTA

He doesn't love me, mother! He doesn't love me! Oh! Listen—he was proscribed by the Council of Venice, that tribunal of death which never pardons; there's a price on his head—well, on a simple indication after a word engraved with a diamond on a mirror, he followed me, mother, he followed me to Venice—whose air must be mortal to him—the daggers of bailiffs, the scaffold on the public square, death hidden, death degrading—he braved all, all for me—does he love me, mother? Do you believe now he loves me?

THEODORA

Poor child.

VIOLETTA

Do you understand now? It's necessary that I leave Venice

instantly, without speaking to him—without any means of making him know where I am! Venice, where he's going to remain alone—proscribed and desperate—and to leave, leave—mother—oh! mother—tell me why it's necessary that we leave?

THEODORA

I don't know myself; it's your father who wishes it, child—he alone can tell you this mystery; explain it to you, this secret only there must be a profound mystery, a terrible secret—for he seemed very agitated, he was quite pale and his voice very altered.

GIOVIANNI

(dully)

Theodora.

THEODORA

Listen, that's him.

GIOVIANNI

(pale, worn out)

Theodora—my daughter—not a minute, not a second to lose—leave—leave!

VIOLETTA

My God!

GIOVIANNI

Leave, I tell you, each minute that slips away is a year—not a word. Not one observation—flee! Flee!

THEODORA

But you are coming with us?

GIOVIANNI

I cannot. My God! Oh! That's what damns me—

THEODORA

But what keeps you in Venice when we are leaving?

GIOVIANNI

An iron chain—a circle of blood—look, woman come—

THEODORA

But—

GIOVIANNI

(taking Violetta in his arms and taking her to the gondola)

Theodora, do you intend to follow your daughter?

THEODORA

Everywhere—everywhere—

GIOVIANNI

(near the gondola)

Then come along—

(calling)

Luigi! Luigi!

SALFIERI

(appearing)

Here I am, Master—

GIOVIANNI

Salfieri! Curses! What are you doing here?

SALFIERI

I'm waiting for you.

GIOVIANNI

(pulling his dagger)

Well, here I am.

VIOLETTA

Salfieri—Father! Father! Mercy!

(throwing herself in the arms of Salfieri)

Mother! Mother! Oh! Why it's Salfieri—help me—protect him—

THEODORA

(pointing to Salfieri)

Him! Him! Defend him! And do you know who he is, this execrable man—

VIOLETTA

What are you saying?

THEODORA

(snatching her from his arms)

Unfortunate girl—he's the Bravo!

VIOLETTA

(hesitating)

Him—him—him—oh! Me—

GIOVIANNI

(taking Violetta by the arm)

Come—come—

SALFIERI

(stopping him by the arm)

Stop.

GIOVIANNI

It's not midnight—

SALFIERI

Listen.

(the first strokes of midnight sound)

GIOVIANNI

I am lost—

SALFIERI

The final hour has struck! It is extinguished. To each his name and his face now—to you this mask and this dagger—to you this order of the Council that you have only an hour to execute.

THEODORA

What do I hear?

SALFIERI

You were mistaken, Theodora, this mask was not made for my face.

(fitting it to the face of Giovianni)

But for his—

THEODORA

Him! You, Giovianni, you—the Bravo!

VIOLETTA

Oh! Then it was you, who—to save your father—

GIOVIANNI

It was I—

VIOLETTA

Oh! Father, my father—!

SALFIERI

You—her father!

VIOLETTA

Oh! Salfieri—oh! Don't condemn him without hearing me—

(She pulls Salfieri aside and speaks to him in a whisper.)

THEODORA

Poor Giovianni—I understand everything now.

GIOVIANNI

Yes, for a moment, I thought that the vengeance of heaven was worn out—I was deceiving myself—the old man, awakened at night in his cell, didn't recognize his son—for the unfortunate is mad—he thought they were coming to take him to the scaffold to assassinate him—and when I wanted to take him in my arms, he clung to the bars of his cell screaming—he screamed, the idiot—and at his screams the guards ran—then I had to leave the old man fainted—dying—for I killed him, perhaps, by trying to save him—I came out—almost mad, almost crazy, myself—urged by the fatal hour—I wanted the two of you to leave—to at least hide my secret from both of you. My daughter's love for Salfieri made this departure even more urgent—for the daughter of the Bravo—

SALFIERI

Violetta has told me everything. Bless your children, for your children love each other, and are asking you to unite them to each other.

THEODORA

What do I hear?

GIOVIANNI

You are a noble young man, Salfieri!

SALFIERI

I love Violetta.

GIOVIANNI

And you swear to marry her?

SALFIERI

I swear it to you, my father, and you know I keep my oaths.

THEODORA

Oh! Thanks, my God.

GIOVIANNI

Well, listen—they are going to leave—leave with them—your vessel is waiting for you in the gulf—you told me—all three of you leave Venice, leave me alone as an accused and desperate man—as I am—

THEODORA

Yes, Giovianni, yes, you are right; leave children—take Violetta to Genoa—wherever you wish, Salfieri, so long as we know where you are and that you love us—

VIOLETTA

Oh, mother—don't abandon us—!

THEODORA

(pointing to the Bravo)

And him, doesn't someone have to remain with him—who suffers with him, who weeps with him—

(she extends her hand to Giovianni)

VIOLETTA

Oh, mother, we will stay also, then.

THEODORA

Poor child! Have you forgotten that your husband is proscribed.

GIOVIANNI

(taking his hand the order of the Council)

Oh! Violetta—you've seen Salfieri deliver this mask and dagger—you've seen this order of the Council given to me, telling me I have only a few moments to execute it—this order—it's a death warrant—I have not opened it yet—I don't yet know the one it's going to strike—but believe me, Violetta take Salfieri away—Salfieri, proscribed and who despite his proscription has dared to put his feet on Venetian territory.

VIOLETTA

You make me tremble? What this order—

GIOVIANNI

That whoever it maybe, it's necessary that I execute it—for the life of my father answers to them for my obedience.

VIOLETTA

Oh! That order—

GIOVIANNI

I am going to have to open it—

VIOLETTA

Ah! Let's flee, Salfieri, let's flee—

(While Violetta is in the arms of Theodora, the Bravo puts on his mask—turning, Violetta utters a scream. Luigi slips under the vestibule.)

BRAVO

(going to Luigi)

Luigi.

LUIGI

Milord, I obeyed, it's past midnight.

BRAVO

These two young people are going to get into the gondola—you will take them out of Venice and you will place them aboard a Levantine ship which is awaiting them at anchor in the gulf—

LUIGI

I will do it, Milord, if the gondola that I met just now that I recognized for certain belonging to the Council of Ten does not prevent me.

BRAVO

The Gondola of the Council? You hear that, Salfieri—no more doubt that they are seeking you, they've ordered me to strike—you have been recognized, denounced, perhaps they even know you are in this house.

THEODORA

Oh! It freezes me with shock—leave children, leave.

BRAVO

Everything is ready. Goodbye.

(Salfieri and Violetta get into the gondola of Luigi who escorts them, singing.)

THEODORA

God give them happiness.

GIOVIANNI

And us courage.

THEODORA

(weeping)

Oh! Yes—oh! My God!

GIOVIANNI

What's wrong with you?

THEODORA

Pardon—it's that order that you have at your belt and that I touched with my hand—

GIOVIANNI

Listen, Theodora—it's a wretched and bloody existence mine is—believe me, before I open this order—this order that shocks you. Our children are not yet far away—rejoin them.

THEODORA

Our children are accomplishing their destiny—let's accomplish ours.

GIOVIANNI

That's fine then.

(opens the order)

Ah!

THEODORA

What's wrong?

GIOVIANNI

Get out of here, Theodora—get out of here—perhaps there's still time. Luigi!

(calling with despair)

THEODORA

Oh! He's too far away now.

(turning)

And the gondola of the Council is very close.

GIOVIANNI

Oh! Why I've read it wrong.

(rereads it)

Why this is atrocious! Oh! Bellamonte! Bellamonte!

THEODORA

What's wrong this time?

What's the matter?

GIOVIANNI

You insulted that man—you called him a coward and infamous—you threw your mask in his face and now this man is avenging himself like a coward and an infamous creature!

THEODORA

And how's that?

GIOVIANNI

Read.

THEODORA

The Council has condemned to death the arsonist, Theodora.

GIOVIANNI

Indeed I told you to leave, Theodora.

THEODORA

Oh! Mercy! Mercy!

(The Bravo and Theodora look at each other, shocked.)

THEODORA

What did I say? Mercy—oh! Don't listen to a cry of the blood, that of a woman—Giovianni—Giovianni—think of your father.

GIOVIANNI

Me! Never! Never!

THEODORA

But your father—they will kill him.

GIOVIANNI

Well, if they kill him, I will be able to die.

THEODORA

Giovianni.

GIOVIANNI

Let this Tribunal of blood do what it wishes—let it kill my father—let it kill me—but me—raise a dagger against you a second time? Me? Impossible; never! Never!

THEODORA

They are approaching—listen, Giovianni—it's better that it be me who dies—look, as for me, I am weary of life—weary of everything. My existence is necessary to no one—God has chosen this expiation; more sorrowful, but more short—what God has done is well done.

GIOVIANNI

This is not the work of God, Theodora; it's the work of men and demons. Tribunal of Murder! Oh! You put this dagger in my hand and said strike—and I will strike.

THEODORA

What are you saying?

GIOVIANNI

I can penetrate into the midst of you, wretches, to strike until my arm is weary—to bathe myself up to my knees in your detested blood—and then—my father dead—I will die—but vengeance at least! Vengeance!

THEODORA

(stopping him in his arms)

Shut up—shut up—if they heard you, my God! For they are there—Giovianni, Giovianni, in the name of heaven, of your father, a poor foolish old geezer. Who's afraid of death like a child—your father—oh! Do you want him dragged to the scaffold by his white hair?

GIOVIANNI

Mercy in my turn, Theodora—mercy! Mercy! Or you will drive me mad.

THEODORA

You've had your expiation in this world—leave mine to me—God intends that my blood purchase that of an old man and wash away my sins—let me, impure woman that I am, let me offer myself in sacrifice since God really wants it.

GIOVIANNI

Despair—

THEODORA

The gondola is stopping—they are there—there—Oh! What can I give in exchange for so much love—which sacrifices all—

(throwing herself into his arms)

I can only give you my life.

(grabbing his dagger from him and stabbing herself)

Since you don't want to take it.

(The bailiff appears here.)

GIOVIANNI

(uttering a scream)

Theodora, what have you done?

BAILIFF

Here he is, Milord.

SENATOR

Giovanni.

THEODORA

Ah! Don't punish him, he has executed the order of the tribunal.

(she expires)

SENATOR

Giovianni, the Republic releases you from your oath—you are free—your father is dead!!

CURTAIN

ABOUT THE AUTHOR

Frank J. Morlock has written and translated many plays since retiring from the legal profession in 1992. His translations have also appeared on Project Gutenberg, the Alexandre Dumas Père web page, Literature in the Age of Napoléon, Infinite Artistries.com, and Munsey's (formerly Blackmask). In 2006 he received an award from the North American Jules Verne Society for his translations of Verne's plays. He lives and works in México.

www.ingramcontent.com/pod-product-compliance
Lightning Source LLC
LaVergne TN
LVHW040115080426
835507LV00039B/373